Ever, *only*, ALL for *Thee*

PAMELA D. BUGDEN

Ever, *only*, ALL for *Thee*

Frances Ridley Havergal:
Glimpses of Her Life and Writings

PAMELA D. BUGDEN

GRANTED
MINISTRIES
— PRESS —

HANNIBAL, MISSOURI
WWW.GRANTEDMINISTRIES.ORG

EVER, *ONLY*, ALL FOR THEE

Copyright © 2009 by Pamela D. Bugden.
Published by Granted Ministries Press, *A Division of Granted Ministries.*

PUBLICATION HISTORY:
1st Edition published in 2007.
2nd Edition published in 2009 by Granted Ministries Press.

Cover design and interior layout by Scott Schaller.
All illustrations, unless otherwise noted, are Copyright ©
The Havergal Trust, 2007.
All rights reserved.

For information or additional copies of *Ever, only, ALL for Thee*
and other resources write:

GRANTED MINISTRIES PRESS
P.O. Box 1348
Hannibal, MO 63401-1348 USA

www.grantedministries.org
orders@grantedministries.org

ISBN 978-0-9817321-7-6
Library of Congress Control Number: 2009938898

Printed in the United States of America
2009

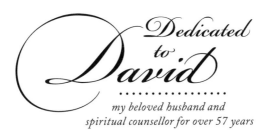

Dedicated to David

*my beloved husband and
spiritual counsellor for over 57 years*

Table of Contents

Foreword

After two or three months into proofreading *The Complete Works of Frances Ridley Havergal* (not yet published), the author realised the value of Havergal's works and desired to share something of the blessing that was there to be received. I have been privileged to be involved in this book as is mentioned in the Preface, and I am very glad to recommend it to readers. As the title suggests, it is only a *glimpse* of her life and works—there is so much more to be discovered as I know through ten years of privileged involvement.

F.R.H. is an example of Jesus Christ's grace and truth shining forth in a life wholly committed to Him. Her devotional life, including a deep study of the word of God, and her desire to tell others of her Master, are well illustrated here.

I am grateful for these 'Glimpses', and want to express thanks also to Pamela's husband, the Rev. David Bugden, for his patience, support and prayers as his wife worked on first *The Complete Works* and then her biography.

– David L. Chalkley, researcher
2007

Publisher's Preface

*A*llow me to give a brief history of my discovery of Frances Ridley Havergal. A few years back I met David Chalkley of Kirksville, Missouri. He was at that time in the midst of the massive task of gathering and arranging all of her extant literature, as well as all relevant information about her. (This work is now nearly completed, and will at some time be published as five volumes, under the title *The Complete Works of Frances Ridley Havergal.*) Frances was a uniquely gifted woman, who used her talents, together with the evident anointing of God upon her labors, for the glory of the great and only King. At the time I met David Chalkley, I knew precious little of F.R.H. I was aware of some of her more well-known hymns, that C.H. Spurgeon thought highly of her (though I did not know he liked to quote from her in his sermons), and that she was included in a book of short biographies on a friend's library shelf.

Mr. Chalkley graciously gave me a copy of each of her five *Royal Books*, as well as *Like a River Glorious*, the massive seed volume for the definitive Havergal edition. It was not two months later that my wife and I were sitting in our living room with friends, each with a different *Royal Book*, reading aloud to one another in turn, joyfully praising God for the truth, simplicity, and power of what we were reading. This began to happen regularly, and such experiences soon created a real appreciation of her value as a Christian writer. Many of her poems and shorter writings were available to me in the seed volume, and I was tremendously blessed by these works, as well as perplexed that Frances was not more well-known today.

As her own preface demonstrates, Pamela Bugden's experience was quite similar to my own—growing in appreciation of Frances as she grew in knowledge of her. It is therefore with gladness that we come together and make Frances' writings, as well as this brief account of her life, more accessible to the Christian public. F.R.H.'s works, all of them, deserve to be widely read and known. In the words of C.H. Spurgeon, she was "the last and loveliest of our modern poets." It is our earnest hope that this book will enlighten the saints of our day to another one of those 'gems' He has given to edify His church throughout her pilgrimage in this world.

– **C.T.** *October*, 2009

Preface

Frances Ridley Havergal (F.R.H.) died at the early age of 42, but the wealth of her writings which she left including hymns, poems and letters is phenomenal. Her work has been described by one who has seen most of this material as a gold mine waiting to be opened up. At the time of her death she was widely known and greatly valued on both sides of the Atlantic, very likely more than four million of her books having been published between 1870 and 1900.

Many readers will have sung at least some of Frances Havergal's hymns over the years, but probably will know very little of her life and works. A lot of these details can be found in her published writings before her death in 1879 and also in her works published posthumously. However, the last significant biography of her was written by Miss Janet Grierson in 1979, which was the centenary of F.R.H.'s death.

In the Foreword to the book by Faith Cook, *Selina, Countess of Huntingdon*, Lady Elizabeth Catherwood writes: 'It is my hope that very many will read this book and discover what God can achieve through a godly woman such as the Countess, whose expressed heart's desire was that "that dear Lamb of God, my best, my eternal, my only Friend should have all dedicated to his service and glory"'.

Frances Havergal was not equal to the Countess in the wide influence she had among ministers and churches in her day, although she was very highly regarded by evangelical ministers in her lifetime (Spurgeon, Horatius Bonar and others). She had the same desire in her own sphere to live to God's glory and to serve Him 'Ever, *only*, ALL for Thee'. Her hymns as well as her writings have been a blessing to very many throughout the world.

In this book the reader is taken through Frances' early days in Worcestershire where her father was rector of Astley Parish Church, and her subsequent life of devotion and service to her Master in various parts of the United Kingdom and abroad. Although she lived in middle-class Victorian England, Frances was never ashamed to be associated with those in need in the local almshouses and the poor cottages in the parish; she also exerted an influence among the higher society of her day. Frances loved to travel and particularly enjoyed being in Switzerland; this book gives accounts of her time there and other places she visited, as well as the story of how some of her hymns came to be written.

I am greatly indebted, more than I can adequately express, to David Chalkley in the USA, whose work in researching all the material on F.R.H. has been monumental. Without his research, resources and ready help, and especially the choice of photographs, this book could never have been written. He has guided the work throughout, making very helpful suggestions and additions, as well as saving me from inaccuracies.

I would also like to thank our granddaughter, Jo Davies, for her involvement in this work and whose computer expertise has been so valuable and necessary.

Perhaps the Rev. Iain Murray did not realise the flood gates he was opening when he suggested to David Chalkley that I might be able to help with proof-reading his work on *The Complete Works of Frances Ridley Havergal*. But I am very grateful for his introduction.

– *Pamela D. Bugden*, 2007

A Summary of the Life of
FRANCES RIDLEY HAVERGAL

1836 14 December	Born at Astley Rectory, Worcestershire
1842	Moved to temporary home at Henwick House, Hallow
1842 5 October	Eldest sister Miriam married Henry Crane
1845	Her father, the Rev. William Henry Havergal, appointed to the Rectory of St. Nicholas, Worcester
1848 5 July	Death of her mother, Mrs. Jane Havergal
1850 August	Went to school at Belmont, a private school for girls near London
1851 Early	Frances converted, made a new creation in Christ. 'I did trust the Lord Jesus.'
1851 July	Father married Caroline Cooke
1852 November	First visit to Germany
1854 17 July	Confirmation in Worcester Cathedral
1856 5 February	Her sister Ellen married Giles Shaw
1856 May	First visit to her sister Ellen & Giles Shaw in Ireland
1860 May	Father resigned living of St Nicholas, Worcester and moved to Shareshill, five and a half miles from Wolverhampton
1861 February	Moved to Oakhampton House to be governess to her two youngest nieces
1866	Shaws returned to England and located to Winterdyne, a large country house near Bewdley, Worcestershire
1867 December	Frances went to stay at Leamington with her father and step-mother
1867 December	First visit to Switzerland with her brother-in-law and family
1869	Publication of her first book, *The Ministry of Song*
1870 19 April	Death of her father

1871 June	Second visit to Switzerland accompanied by her close friend Elizabeth Clay
1873 Summer	Third visit to Switzerland with the Rev. and Mrs. Charles B. Snepp
1874 August	Fourth visit to Switzerland with her sister Miriam and brother-in-law Henry Crane, and their daughter Constance
1875 January	Her brother Henry East dies
1876 6 July	Final visit to Switzerland with her sister Maria
1877	A stay at Mildmay Conference Centre
1877	Publication of her first Royal Book, *My King*
1878 26 May	Death of her stepmother and break up of the home in Leamington
1878 October	Joined Maria at the home in Mumbles near Swansea, Wales
1879 January	Final visit to her publishers in London
1879 3 June	Frances' death and entry into her King's presence
1879 9 June	Buried in Astley Churchyard

Chapter One

A Happy Home

A HAPPY HOME

O happy home where Thou art loved the dearest,
　Thou loving Friend and Saviour of our race;
And where among the guests there never cometh
　One who can hold such high and honoured place!

O happy home where each one serves Thee, lowly,
　Whatever his appointed work may be,
Till every common task seems great and holy,
　When it is done, O Lord, as unto Thee!

O happy home, where Thou art not forgotten
　When joy is overflowing, full and free;
O happy home, where every wounded spirit
　Is brought, Physician, Comforter, to Thee.

C. J. P. Spitta, trans. Sarah L. Findlater

A few months before Queen Victoria came to the throne, Frances Ridley Havergal was born on December 14, 1836 at Astley rectory in Worcestershire where her father, the Rev. William Henry Havergal, was rector. She was the youngest of six children—Miriam, Maria and Ellen were 19, 15 and 13 when she was born; her brothers Henry and Frank were 16 and 7. Her mother was known as 'the lovely Jane Head'.

Speaking of home life at Astley, Maria said, 'God's everlasting love might be the shining motto of those happy days...with a father never too strict, never too indulgent; with a mother teaching us thrifty elegance in our dress, and self-helping habit, order and cheerfulness—a truly merry and happy household were we.'

Engraved by E. Evans.

S.E. VIEW OF ASTLEY CHURCH AND RECTORY
From a sketch by Miriam Havergal, 1839

The rectory, which stood on high ground beside the church, commanded a wonderful view of the surrounding countryside. To the south, outlined against the sky, stretched the distant range of the Malverns, their pale blue haze suggesting mystery and calm. In the middle distance stood the graceful tree-clad hills of Woodbury and Abberley; and immediately below was undulating land, neatly parcelled out into fields, orchards, plantations, woods and copses.

The thirty to forty acres of land adjacent to the rectory was a paradise for children, and Frances especially loved the wild woodland garden just below the church, which her father had landscaped on the site of an old monastic vineyard when he first came to Astley. A connoisseur of trees, he had planted it with specimens of unusual interest, including cedars, walnuts, weeping beeches, giant redwood and silver fir, the biggest of its kind. Frances used to scamper along the labyrinthine paths, down through the trees to her favourite flower-carpeted dell which lay alongside Dick Brook.

The lure of tree-climbing sometimes checked her progress, but more often she made straight for the brook where Flora, her faithful little white and tan spaniel, could seek out her special haunts, while her young mistress helped herself to fistfuls of violets, snowdrops, primroses, or whatever enticing flowers happened to be in season.

Daily life at the rectory was for Frances a mixed experience of freedom and restriction. There was ample space for play as no attempt was made to confine her to the nursery, but she had to learn the discipline of life in a well-regulated household. With her mercurial temperament—her father often called her 'Little Quicksilver'—this could have been difficult at times.

Family prayers were the first big event of the day, and from the time she was a toddler Frances joined in: it was the tradition for the youngest to sit on father's knee. Sundays provided her with the additional privilege of taking round the missionary collecting plate to the assembled household. This included not only members of the family, but also the resident servants, and her father's pupils, whose numbers varied at any given time from two to six. Each week the money was transferred to a Church Missionary Society box, which once a year was given a ceremonial opening. Great was the excitement of the children as they watched the growing piles of halfpennies, pennies and even occasional shillings, usually reckoning the grand total of £4–£5.

Sunday was far from being a dull day. The extra excitement of the missionary collection at breakfast time was matched in the evening by a session of hymn singing, led by Mr. Havergal, who was already a composer of some repute in the field of church music, besides being an excellent singer. As he sat by his seraphine (precursor of the harmonium) accompanying the hymns, it was Frances' favourite game to clamber up on his shoulder and make her own contribution to proceedings from this exalted music stool.

Frances was too young when she was at Astley to see much of her father's day-to-day work in the parish. To the extent that his health permitted, he pursued a quiet unobtrusive life of a country rector, allotting first place in his daily routine to the visitation of his parishioners, especially the sick and poor. Occasionally the older children were allowed to accompany him on his visits, and this enabled Frances' sister Miriam to speak of them from firsthand observation:

> We saw how kindly he shook hands, how gentle his ways, and then he
> felt the invalid's pulse and saw about the medicine, for he was skilful,

and the parish doctor thanked him for saving him visits; and then he read to them Bible comfort, and prayed.

Mrs. Havergal, who supported her husband in all his work and especially in visiting the cottagers, often took Frances with her. She would help to carry the basket of new-laid eggs, or a can of soup or milk, or even one of the delicious apple turnovers that came hot from the rectory kitchen. In a cottage of some sick parishioner Frances would help to mind the baby while her mother attended to whatever skilled nursing was required. It was from these experiences that Frances' own ministry to the poor and needy was developed.

– Education –

Mrs. Havergal and her eldest daughter Miriam took charge of Frances' formal education. Each morning she learnt reading, spelling and a rhyme. While still under three, this instruction lasted for only half an hour, to be followed in the afternoon by a session on patchwork-stitching and the learning of a short text which had to be repeated next morning at breakfast. By the age of three she could read easy books, and her brother would often find her hiding under a table engrossed in a story. French and music were soon added to the curriculum. Her keenness to learn was so great that it had to be controlled rather than encouraged, for there were times when the excitement of widening horizons was liable to overtax her strength. At the age of seven she began to scribble hymns, and from nine onwards she would write fluent letters in rhyme to her friends.

– Religious Impressions –

When in later life Frances started to write an autobiography, she commenced with her recollections of herself and her surroundings when she was four years old. She writes:

> Up to the time that I was six years old I have no remembrance of any religious ideas whatever. Even when taken once to see the corpse of a little boy of my own age (four years) lying in a coffin strewn with flowers, in dear papa's parish of Astley, I did not think about it as otherwise than a very sad and very curious thing that that little child should lie so still and cold…But from six to eight I recall a different state of things.

The beginning of it was a sermon preached one Sunday morning at Hallow Church, near Worcester, by Mr. (now Archdeacon) Philpotts. Of this I even now retain a distinct impression. It was to me a very terrible one, dwelling much on hell and judgment, and what a fearful thing it is to fall into the hands of the living God. No one ever knew it, but this sermon haunted me, and day and night it crossed me. I began to pray a good deal, though only night and morning, with a sort of fidget and impatience, almost angry at feeling so unhappy, and wanting and expecting a new heart and have everything put straight and be made happy, all at once.

All this time she could not bear being 'talked to', or prayed with, though she kept up a custom of going by herself every Sunday afternoon to a quiet room, and after reading a chapter in the New Testament would kneel down and pray, after which she 'usually felt soothed and less naughty'.

- New Surroundings -

In 1842 the living of Astley was resigned, and Henwick House, in the parish of Hallow, was the temporary family home until Mr. Havergal was appointed rector of St. Nicholas, Worcester, in 1845. She writes: 'We went to St. Nicholas' Rectory in 1845, and it was in very great bitterness that I bade adieu to my pleasant country life, and became, as I remember dear papa calling me, "a caged lark"'. One consolation of this move was, however, that she had a tiny room all her own with a window that enabled her to appreciate the sky and clouds in the same way that trees and flowers had been her joy at Henwick.

Soon after their arrival in Worcester, a sermon by the curate on the text 'Fear not, little flock' aroused her from the feeling of self–satisfaction into which she had drifted. Having a favourable opportunity, she unburdened her heart one evening to the curate, but he did not help the young seeker. He said the excitement of moving and coming into new scenes was most likely the cause of her feeling worse, and that it would soon go off, and then she was to try and be a good girl and pray. So after that her lips were utterly sealed to all but God for another few years.

This inner sadness, however, did not prevent Frances from realising the situation of other children who were not as favoured as she was. She was concerned about those in her Sunday School class who were in need and at the age of nine decided to do something about it. Enlisting the aid of her friend, young Sophie Sadler, daughter of Michael Thomas Sadler, M.P., she established the Flannel Petticoat Society for the clothing of these children. From August to October every year they collected subscriptions from their friends, ranging from 3 pence to 1/- [one shilling]. Frances' mother was chief adviser on shopping and dressmaking, while her sisters Maria and Ellen were deputed to select the children. November 5th was the highlight of the Society's year. On that day a motley band of children, some twenty-five to thirty strong, invaded the rectory, exchanged their rags for brand new carefully fitted garments, and then celebrated the occasion with hymn singing and a slice of cake!

ST. NICHOLAS' CHURCH, WORCHESTER
From a Sketch taken in 1848.

St. Nicholas' parish had its share of Almshouses and several of them came under the care of Canon Havergal. One of these, known as the Trinity Almshouses, was where Frances and her sister Maria were welcome visitors; Maria has written an interesting account of the building and some of its occupants in her book *Pleasant Fruits*. Frances herself felt that she had not been as diligent as she should have been, commenting that 'My dear almshouse folks are so affectionate…it smites me rather, because I feel it more than I deserve'. But from conversations recorded in *Pleasant Fruits* it is evident that 'our dear Miss Fanny' was a most welcome visitor. As ninety-five year old Mary Hart said: 'I like her step on my floor, and the sun seems to shine in her face, and she's always welcome to poor Mary Hart'; her musical contribution to the old people's New Year party was something that was particularly appreciated.

- A Sad Event -

In 1848 Frances' mother became seriously ill, and feeling that she was soon to leave her little girl, she said to her one evening: 'Fanny dear, pray to God to prepare you for all that He is preparing for you'. This sad event, which the mother thus anticipated, Frances could not or would not understand. Frances would later write of the grief she suffered watching from the window as the funeral procession passed from the rectory to the churchyard, and the anguish she felt in her little heart, and uttering the lonely cry of a motherless heart, 'Oh, mamma! mamma! mamma!'. Her bright and apparently thoughtless manner led some to think that she was heartless, but all the while she was heavy and sad for her loss, and weary because she had not yet found pardon for her sin.

- New Horizons -

A fresh chapter opened when at the age of 13 Frances was sent to a boarding school for girls in London where the Principal, Mrs. Teed, had in her care more than a hundred pupils at 'Belmont', near Campden Hill. The spiritual influences of school deepened and intensified the religious teaching which she had received at home. She says of that time, 'That single half-year was perhaps the most important to me of any in my life', though her longing for assurance remained unfulfilled. But Frances tells of how, soon after her fourteenth birthday, she remembers talking to Miss Caroline Cooke, who had become a good friend, and who later became her stepmother:

> I told her again how I longed to know that I was forgiven. She asked me a question which led to the hearty answer that I was sure I desired it above everything on earth, that even my precious papa was nothing in comparison...After a few more words she said 'Why cannot you trust yourself to your Saviour at once? Supposing that now, at this moment, Christ were to come in the clouds of heaven, and take up His redeemed, could you not trust Him? Would not His call, His promise, be enough for you? Could you not commit your soul to Him, to your Saviour, Jesus?' Then came a flash of hope across me, which made me feel literally breathless. I remember how my heart beat. 'I could surely', was my response; and I left her suddenly and ran away upstairs to think it out. I flung myself on my knees in my room, and strove to realize the sudden hope. I was very happy at last. I could commit my soul to Jesus. I did not, and need not, fear His coming. I could trust Him with my all for eternity...Then and there, I committed my soul to the Saviour... and earth and heaven seemed bright from that moment—I did trust the Lord Jesus.

- *Changes in the Family Home* -

In 1851 Frances' father married Caroline Cooke. In the autumn of 1852, they took Frances to Germany, where Mr. Havergal, whose eyes had long troubled him, spent the winter under the care of a skilful oculist at Dusseldorf. Here Frances attended the Louisenschule, with excellent results. She studied ardently, and even 'began to think in German'. When the school year ended in the summer of 1853, she was given First Prize among the school's 110 students -a wonderful achievement by this English girl of sixteen, and never before done in a foreign school. Years later she studied in the home of her German master, Pastor Schulze-Berge, who wrote of her:

> She showed from the first such application, such rare talent, such depth of comprehension, that I can only speak of her progress as extraordinary. She acquired a knowledge of our most celebrated authors in a short time as even German ladies attain only after much longer study.

For some months longer she went on studying at Obercassel. Situated on the east bank of the Rhine, not far from Bonn and

65km from Dusseldorf, Obercassel was in the region of the Seven Mountains and enjoyed a fine view of the famous Drachenfels. Frances, a lover of the countryside, was delighted to exchange the urban elegance of Dusseldorf for the lush meadows and the attractions of river and mountains. Before Christmas of that year Frances returned with her parents to Worcester.

– An Important Occasion –

In 1854 Frances was confirmed in Worcester Cathedral; this was of considerable significance to her, the public profession being a very real act. When asked by the bishop the solemn question to which all have audibly to answer, 'I do', the reply of her heart was 'Lord, I cannot without Thee; but oh, with Thy almighty help, I do'. She always marked the anniversary of it by spending much time in prayer, reading and meditation. A poem she wrote on the day itself, later published by her sister, shows her thoughts:

"THINE FOR EVER"

Oh! "Thine for ever," what a blessed thing
To be for ever His who died for me!
My Saviour, all my life Thy praise I'll sing,
Nor cease my song throughout eternity.

(*Memorials of Frances Ridley Havergal*)

Although Frances had felt like a 'caged lark' in her early days in Worcester, she had thrown herself so wholeheartedly into the life of the parish that when the time came to leave she felt the parting almost as deeply as Canon Havergal himself. But his failing health had prevented him from fulfilling the tasks of a busy city parish, and when, in 1859, he received the offer of a very small rural living in Shareshill in the diocese of Lichfield, he accepted it and went there in March 1860. For Frances, the closing of one door where she had been so happy and active in Sunday School work and visitation was the opening of another. Through an invitation to contribute poems to a magazine, *Good Words*, she realised that the pen was to be one of the instruments through which she was to exercise a ministry.

- A Postscript -

When Frances received her first cheque from the publishers for her contributions to *Good Words*, she wrote the following to her stepmother in 1863:

> The cheque is so much larger than I expected, £10.17s. 6d. Now will you please give £10 of this to my precious papa for anything he would like to employ it on; either keep it for church alterations, or if any more immediate and pressing object, I would rather he used it for that; I should be so delighted to be able for once to further any little object which he may desire. I should be glad if you would send 10s. to J.H.E. for the Scripture Readers' collection, and the 7s.6d. to keep for any similar emergency.

This note was found among Frances' papers later:

> My dear little Fan can hardly think how much her poor papa loves her, thinks about her, and prays for her Yes, he does. Thank you, dear child, for remembering me; I will keep all your love, but not the cheque. Our God send you His sweetest and choicest blessings.

– William Henry Havergal

Chapter Two

A Visit to Ireland

While the Havergal family were still at St. Nicholas' Church in Worcester, Frances' older sister Ellen married a widower, Giles Shaw. He was proprietor of flax and corn mills in Celbridge, a village on the banks of the Liffey, some twelve miles west of Dublin. Because of the concern he had for the welfare of his five hundred employees he was loved and respected by the workers. Ellen quickly adapted to her new life and shared in that concern.

Celbridge Lodge, the home of Giles and Ellen, was a typical Irish country house of the early Victorian period, and it was in May 1856 that Frances made her first visit there. As she was driven through the main gates, past the little lodge and up the shady avenue, with the beeches in their spring green giving her the appropriate welcome of the Emerald Isle, she must have wondered what new experiences awaited her in this as yet unknown country.

One of her earliest interests was the Charter School, which was situated not far from Celbridge Lodge. In 1809 this establishment had been given to the Incorporated Society for Promoting English Protestant Schools in Ireland, and drew its pupils from a wide area. On Sunday evenings the older girls, with their Headmistress, used to come to Celbridge Lodge where they would be welcomed by Ellen in the beautiful entrance hall and taken into the drawing-room for their weekly Bible class. One of these girls later recalled her first impression of Frances who was then nineteen:

> In a few seconds Miss Frances, carolling like a bird, flashed into the room! Flashed! Yes, I say the word advisedly, flashed like a burst of

sunshine, like a hillside breeze, and stood before us, her fair sunny curls falling round her shoulders, her bright eyes dancing and her fresh sweet voice ringing through the room. I shall never forget that afternoon, never! I sat perfectly spellbound as she sang chant and hymn with marvellous sweetness, and then played two or three pieces of Handel, which thrilled me through and through. She shook hands with each, and said with a merry laugh: 'the next time I come to Ireland I think we must get up a little singing class, and then you know you must all sing with me'!

Frances kept her word, and on the next visit, which was a longer one, she formed a singing class for the girls. Years later, one of them, destitute and dying in a workhouse hospital, recalled many instances of the kindness of the Shaws at Celbridge Lodge, and one of her special memories was of this singing class:

> Those were happy days, but my greatest treat was coming up to Miss F.H.'s little singing class in the drawing-room. That was music. We used to sing 'Jerusalem, my happy home', and that's where I am fast going now.

- The Irish Society -

Giles Shaw was treasurer of the Irish Society and one day during her first visit to their home, Frances had accompanied him to a committee meeting, and was given such a stirring report of the activities of the Society that she took a collecting card for the cause. Beginning with a £1 contribution in 1856, she had by March 1869 sent in over £500. The Society, founded in 1818, aimed at 'the Scriptural Education of the Irish-speaking Population, chiefly through the medium of their own language'. Nearly a million and a half of the population was Irish-speaking and many were illiterate, so besides supplying copies of the Scriptures in Irish, the Society had to encourage people to commit passages to memory and also provide Irish-speaking teachers to help them to read.

The taking of that collecting card was the beginning of Frances' involvement in the work of the Irish Society, and the cause soon had her full support. On her return home to Worcester she determined to raise interest in the Society. Canon Havergal fully supported his daughter's efforts, and she writes to Ellen: 'My father gave the Irish

Society a capital introduction last Sunday in the sermon; it will not be his fault if collections are small'.

In 1859, with her father's help, she organised a branch society in Worcester, launching it with a public meeting at the Guildhall addressed by the Rev. Thomas Moriarty who had been at one time a powerful opponent of the work of the Irish Society. Frances wrote a sketch in which she tells of how Tom tried hard to disrupt a meeting in Dingle that was to be addressed in Irish by a Dublin clergyman, but who was remarkably converted from Romanism and became a fruitful missionary in a remote Irish-speaking part of the country.

At that meeting there was a young girl known by her pet name 'Bruey' who became Frances' first collector for the Irish Society. The story of Bruey is told in a book bearing her name written by Frances which, by 1883, had a circulation of 34,000. It has been rated as one of Frances' best children's books.

The outline of the story is true. One of the child's names was Bruce, hence her pet name of Bruey; the sketch of her character is founded on recollections and incidents. Her work for the Irish Society, her illness and peaceful death are all facts. Because Bruey was her first collector, Frances called it the Bruey Branch.

Frances Havergal was always prepared to face her critics, and a few months before she died she wrote to the readers of Bruey:

> I am sometimes remonstrated with for 'making Bruey die'...The answer is, I didn't make her die; she did die, and I could not help the fact. Had I been writing a fiction, I should have made her go to the seaside and collect [contributions for the Irish Society], and 'live happily ever after', as the fairy tales say. But dear little Bruey's collecting was no fiction, nor her calm, happy death. Names and persons are disguised throughout, but all the facts are quite real...It struck me you might really find it useful to be able to assure people that Bruey was a 'real little girl'.

In March 1879 Frances wrote that she was 'almost frightened at the rate the Bruey Branch is growing': the collectors were faithful in sending their cards with the money they had gathered. In the year of Frances' death there were over one hundred collectors who had raised £850 16s. 9d. She had been planning a trip to Ireland, to observe the mission's works first hand and then to write about them.

She had been scheduled to leave on June 4 but died just the day before aged 42.

On June 10, 1879 the Committee of the Irish Society paid this tribute to Frances after her death was announced a few days previously:

> Her death is a serious loss to the Irish Society, for which she had been an indefatigable collector and advocate, for which she had written her popular little book Bruey, and established the Juvenile Branch called the 'Bruey' Branch, and for which she was about to undertake a tour of visits to its mission stations in Ireland, with the intention of writing sketches of her tour, when it pleased God to take her to Himself.

In 1882 the work of the Bruey Branch was still ongoing, and a letter from the Earl of Shaftesbury to the Hon. Secretaries shows his estimate of the work:

> ...If I can do any good to the *Bruey Banch* of the late admirable Frances Ridley Havergal, and show any respect thereby to the memory of that inestimable woman, I shall be most happy to become a Patron.

A little while after F.R.H.'s death the Irish Society decided to purchase the Masonic Hall in Limerick and name it 'The Havergal Memorial Hall' with the intention that it would be used for mission services, sermons or addresses in Irish, ragged and mission schools (Sunday and weekday) etc. The Boys' Ragged School and the Girls' and Infant Schools provided shelter and education for the children of the very poorest class. A report of the progress of this work, made shortly after the completion of the building under the management of Canon Gregg, stated that the number on school rolls was 185 and resident in dormitories, 122. Many who had been cared for in these schools joined the Navy, some were sent to the Church of Ireland Training College to be trained as teachers; nearly all were in respectable independence, who but for these admirable Schools might have been added to the number of the criminal population.

PRAYER FOR IRELAND

Gracious Saviour, look in mercy on this Island of the West,
Win the wandering and the weary with Thy pardon and Thy rest;
As the only Friend and Saviour let Thy blessed Name be owned,
Who hast shed Thy blood most precious, and for ever hast atoned.

Oh, surround Thy throne of power with Thine emerald bow of peace;
Bid the wailing and the warring and the wild confusion cease.
Thou remainest King for ever; Thou shalt reign, and earth adore!
Thine the kingdom, Thine the power, Thine the glory evermore.

(first and fourth stanzas; *Lilies and Shamrocks*)

- The Shaws Return to England -

The cholera epidemic that swept Ireland in the early autumn of 1866 hit Celbridge particularly badly. Unlike two doctors who had fled the district, Giles and his eldest son John, together with another doctor, put all their energies into fighting the plague. Besides supplying medical help, Giles and John provided necessary provision for their mill workers as well as arranging for food and clothing to the needy in the neighbourhood.

For various reasons, having seen the cholera epidemic through, Giles decided to return to England whilst his son John, having taken first-class honours in Divinity at Trinity College, Dublin in 1865, was beginning to think about the possibility of ordination. At this time, Winterdyne, a beautiful country house near Bewdley became available to rent. It was purchased when it came on the open market in 1870, to the great delight of the family. It was not too far from Shareshill, where Frances' father and stepmother lived, and was also situated near the Cranes in Oakhampton House, the home of Frances' oldest sister Miriam and her husband Henry Crane.

Frances knew that she could always be sure of a warm welcome to this hospitable home, and Ellen's four children were all of an age to appeal to an aunt who felt especially at ease with young children. For a short time in 1868 she was their governess. She said, 'I got fonder than ever of the children and they of me too—I quite enjoyed teaching them, and they were so loving and docile that it was all pleasure'.

One of Frances' popular children's books, *Ben Brightboots*, is based on what happened to the Shaws' tabby kitten and its offspring, and it also depicts vividly the lovely grounds and happy home life at Winterdyne.

Frances wrote several of her hymns whilst staying in these peaceful surroundings, including the following written in 1874:

ANOTHER YEAR

Another year is dawning!
  Dear Master, let it be,
In working or in waiting,
  Another year with Thee.

Another year of leaning
  Upon Thy loving breast,
Of ever-deepening trustfulness,
  Of quiet, happy rest.

Another year of mercies,
  Of faithfulness and grace;
Another year of gladness
  In the shining of Thy face.

Another year of progress,
  Another year of praise;
Another year of proving
  Thy presence 'all the days'.

Another year of service,
  Of witness for Thy love;
Another year of training
  For holier work above.

Another year is dawning,
  Dear Master, let it be,
On earth, or else in heaven,
  Another year for Thee!

(*The Complete Poetical Works of Frances Ridley Havergal*)

Chapter Three

The Ministry of Song

This writer has a set of three books by F.R.H.—*The Ministry of Song, Under the Surface* and *'Under His Shadow'*. They are pocket-sized, beautifully bound and in a neat cloth case. When they were published in the 1870s the set sold for six shillings. It cost £12.50 in 2005! These are some stanzas from her first poem in *The Ministry of Song*:

THE MINISTRY OF SONG

In God's great field of labour
    All work is not the same;
He hath a service for each one
    Who loves His holy name.
And you, to whom the secrets
    Of all sweet sounds are known,
Rise up! For He hath called you
    To a mission of your own.
And, rightly to fulfil it,
    His grace can make you strong,
Who to your charge hath given
    The Ministry of Song.

Sing to the little children,
    And they will listen well;
Sing grand and holy music,
    For they can feel its spell…

I remember, late one evening,
    How the music stopped, for, hark!
Charlie's nursery door was open,
    He was calling in the dark,—
'Oh, no! I am not frightened,
    And I do not want a light;
But I cannot sleep for thinking
    Of the song you sang last night.
Something about a "valley",
    And "make rough places plain",
And "Comfort ye"; so beautiful!
    Oh, sing it me again!'

(first three stanzas; *The Ministry of Song*)

Frances' first published book was *The Ministry of Song* printed in 1869 by the Christian Book Society of London. Her original inscription was 'To My Father'. After he died in 1870 the inscription 'To my Father's Memory' was placed at the front of the book when Nisbet published it in 1871.

Reading through these books one comes across gems which catch the eye. This is from *Under the Surface*:

THE SOVEREIGNTY OF GOD

In Thy sovereignty rejoicing, we Thy children bow and praise,
For we know that kind and loving, just and true, are all Thy ways.
While Thy heart of sovereign mercy, and Thine arm of sovereign might,
For our great and strong salvation in Thy sovereign grace unite.

(third stanza; *Under the Surface)*

C.H. Spurgeon was familiar with many of Frances' writings, and the following extract relating to '*Under His Shadow*' was in an address found in *Till He Come: Communion Meditations*:

I must confess of my short discourse, as the man did of the axe which fell into the stream, that it is borrowed. The outline of it is taken from one who will never complain of me, for to the great loss of the Church she has left these lower choirs to sing above. Miss Havergal, last and loveliest of our modern poets, when her tones were most mellow and her language most sublime, has been caught up to swell the music of heaven. Her last poems are published with the title *Under His Shadow*, and the preface gives the reason for the name. She said, 'I should like the title to be, *Under His Shadow*. I seem to see four pictures suggested by that: under the shadow of a rock, in a weary plain; under the shadow of a tree; closer still, under the shadow of His wing; nearest and closest, in the shadow of His hand. Surely that hand must be the pierced hand, that may oftentimes press us sorely, and yet evermore encircling, upholding, and shadowing'.

Spurgeon goes on:

> *Under His Shadow* is our afternoon subject, and we will in a few words enlarge on the Scriptural plan which Miss Havergal has bequeathed to us. Our text is, 'He that dwelleth in the secret place of the Most High shall abide under the shadow of the Almighty'.

He proceeds with an exposition of Psalm 91:1 under the four headings mentioned above.

The esteem in which Spurgeon held Frances was obviously mutual. On one occasion she heard Spurgeon preach, and she commented:

> Magnificent! I don't recollect ever hearing anything finer...That 'Tabernacle' is certainly one of the most remarkable sights in the world—the end of the season and London half empty, but it was thronged, and always is, twice every Sunday; and more than half are men, and intellectual-looking too.

Frances Havergal was known as 'the sweet singer' and loved to sing wherever she was. Regarding a visit to Colwyn, North Wales in August 1852, we have this comment, recorded by her sister Maria in *Memorials of Frances Ridley Havergal*:

> We find pretty walks *ad infinitum*. The donkey-girl teaches me Welsh. I think I learn it very fast, and I have a Welsh Testament and Prayer Book. At what Mary [her companion] calls the 'Taffy Service' I can sing and chant and respond as fully as the natives themselves...

As Welsh is the only tonal language in the West it is not the easiest to learn!

Frances was never one to be beaten. Her linguistic ability enabled her to sing in French when in Switzerland and in German when staying with Pastor Schulze-Berge. On another occasion when in Ormont Dessus in Switzerland, she was in a village church and wrote of this experience:

The people sing beautifully, a downright treat, in German choral style as to music, slow rich harmonies that bear dwelling on...It was such sweet singing, every one keeping to cres. and dim., neither instrument nor any stated choir, but all the parts correctly sung by the congregation of peasants.

When Maria returned to Switzerland for a holiday after Frances' death, the people who had known her remembered 'her sweet voice echoing through the mountainside'.

This is an excerpt from a letter Frances wrote to her publisher in 1876:

I must tell you a wonderful bit of *Ministry of Song*, through 'Whom having not seen, ye love'. I was taken on speculation to call on a clever young gentleman, just an infidel, knowing the Bible and disbelieving it, and believing that nobody else really believes, but that religion is all humbug and mere profession. I was not primed at all, only knew that he was 'not a religious man'. In the first place, I had no end of fun with him, and got on thoroughly good terms—then was asked to sing. I prayed the whole time I was singing, and felt God very near and helping me. After a Handel song or two which greatly delighted him, I sang 'Tell it out!', felt the glorious truth that He is King, and couldn't help breaking off in the very middle and saying so, right out!

Then I sang, 'Whom having not seen, ye love' and felt as if I could sing out all the love of my heart in it. Well, this young infidel, who had seemed extremely surprised and subdued by 'Tell it out!', completely broke down and went away to hide his tears in a bay window. And afterwards we sat down together, and he let me 'tell it out' as I pleased, and it was not hard to speak of Him of whom I had sung. He seemed altogether struck and subdued, and listened like a child. He said, 'Well there is faith then, you have it anyhow—I saw it when you sang, and I could not stand it, and that's the fact!' He was anxious for me to come again.

When I came away, his sister, who had introduced me, wept for joy, saying she had persuaded me to come with a vague hope that he 'might find he could tolerate a religious person', but never dared to hope such an effect as this, and that she thought I had been most marvellously guided in drawing the bow at a venture, for every word and even action had been just right...I should add that it was almost a miracle in another way, for I had such a wretched cold that I doubted being able to sing at all, and yet I believe I never sang clearer and better and stronger. How good God is!

In 1842 Frances' sister Miriam had married Henry Crane, a landowner with a large estate at Oakhampton in Astley parish. Frances was to be a frequent visitor there, calling it the 'home of roses', with its spacious house and grounds. Having the oversight of a 250-300 acre estate and a family of four children to care for, it was obvious that Henry and Miriam could do with help. So when looking for a governess for Evelyn (8) and Constance (7) why should it not be 'Aunt Fanny' who was already popular with the household? Thus from 1860-67 Frances lived mostly in Oakhampton House, with breaks for visiting friends and relatives, and a few weeks' holiday from time to time.

Although there were not the opportunities for service that she had had in Worcester, she quickly found other avenues for her gifts, such as Sunday school teaching, evening classes for girls and visiting the cottagers.

Also, whilst with the family, her brother-in-law Henry had arranged for her to have singing lessons with Dr. William Marshall, who conducted the Kidderminster Philharmonic Society. Towards the end of her stay at Oakhampton House she received a series of singing lessons in London with Alberto Randegger, a composer, conductor and professor of singing at the Royal Academy of Music. When required to write an abstract of her first singing lesson, she astonished her instructor by producing it in verse:

MY SINGING LESSON

The voice has machinery—(now to be serious),
Invisible, delicate, strange and mysterious.
A wonderful organ-pipe firstly we trace,
Which is small in a tenor and wide in a bass;
Below an Aeolian harp is provided,
Through whose fairy-like fibres the air will be guided.
Above is an orifice, larger or small
As the singer desires to rise or to fall;
Expand and depress it to deepen your roar,
But raise and contract it when high you would soar.

In the feminine voice there are registers three,
Which upper, and middle, and lower must be;
And each has a sounding board all of its own,
The chest, lips, and head, to reverberate tone.
But in cavities nasal it never must ring,
Or no one is likely to wish you to sing.
And if on this subject you waver in doubt,
By listening and feeling the truth will come out.
The lips, by the bye, will have plenty to do
In forming the vowels, Italian and true;
Eschewing the English, uncertain and hideous,
With an O and a U that are simply amphibious
In flexible freedom let both work together,
And the under one must not be stiffened like leather.

Here endeth the substance of what I remember,
Indited this twenty-sixth day of November.

(partial quotation; *Complete Poetical Works*)

Randegger was pleased with her poem on his lessons, showed it to many others, and asked Frances to provide him with texts by her that he could set to music. She gave him twelve poems for children, which were published with his music as *Sacred Songs for Little Singers*. These were dedicated, by the gracious permission of Her Majesty (Queen Victoria), to Her Royal Highness, the Princess Beatrice, January 1870.

Frances would sing anywhere and at any time but it would always be for her Master. There was one occasion when she was visiting her friends, the Rev. and Mrs. Charles B. Snepp at Perry Barr:

> Dr. Marshall sent me the programme of the next Kidderminster concert and strongly urged me to sing the part of Jezebel in the 'Elijah', saying that he could not depend on anyone else for it. I knew I could do it; for once, at the practice, the doctor said I threw such life into it. Mentioning it to Mr. Snepp, he expressed surprise, and his words struck me: 'How can a Christian girl personate Jezebel?' So I thought about it, saw the inconsistency, and gave it up.

During a visit to London, Frances was invited to an amateur musical evening concerning which her sister Maria wrote:

> Some classical music was rendered and F. was especially riveted by the finished singing of an Italian lady. Presently my sister was invited,

last of all, to the piano. True to her resolve, 'Let me sing only, always for my King', she chose a song of Handel's. Then the hostess gracefully pressed for one of her own compositions: so she sang, 'Whom having not seen, ye love'....The rooms were hushed; and then the Italian stranger, with tears in her eyes, sought her as she left the piano, with, 'Miss Havergal, I envy you; your words and face tell me you have something I have not'.

This lady knew well Princess Beatrice, the daughter of Queen Victoria, and Frances expressed a wish that her book *Life Mosaic* should be given to her. This was done and a gracious reply was received from the Princess, with a royal signature beneath her photo. Frances treasured that for the rest of her life. On another occasion Frances writes:

> I was at a large regular London party...and of course I sang 'for Jesus', and did not I have dead silence? Afterwards I had two really important conversations with strangers; one seemed extremely surprised at finding himself quite easily drifted from the badinage with which he started into a right-down personal talk about his personal danger and his only hope for safety; he took it very well, and thanked me. Perhaps the seed may bear fruit.

In answer to the inquiry, 'Who is Fanny Crosby?', Frances replied: 'She is a blind lady, whose heart can see splendidly in the sunshine of God's love'. One verse of her poem to the 'sweet blind singer over the sea' is quoted below:

A SEEING HEART

Dear blind sister over the sea!
An English heart goes forth to thee.
We are linked by a cable of faith and song,
Flashing bright sympathy swift along;
One in the East and one in the West,
Singing for Him who our souls love best,
'Singing for Jesus', telling His love
All the way to our home above,
Where the severing sea, with its restless tide,
Never shall hinder, and never divide.
Sister! What will our meeting be,
When our hearts shall sing and our eyes shall see!

(last stanza; *Under the Surface*)

A month or so before Frances died she was invited to go to a meeting in nearby Swansea. On the way she said to her travelling companion that she 'felt as if she had no right to go teaching others—such a sinner as I am; but then Mary, I am just trusting for every word'. Her subject was Hosea 3—'I also for thee'. The hymn that had been chosen was not felt by Frances to be suitable so she asked if they could sing 'Precious Saviour, may I live, only for Thee'. When told they did not know her tune 'Onesimus' to it, she replied: 'No fear! Do let me just sing one verse alone, and I know they will join.' She went to the piano and sang one verse, and then all the rest joined in heartily.

Her sister Maria wrote of this occasion:

> It seems to have been a great night of decision to many present. The next morning before ever her breakfast was finished, one and another came for conversation...a French governess was specially impressed.

Even though this meeting exhausted her, she welcomed any opportunity to speak for her King:

EIGHTEENTH DAY

> What shall be our word for Jesus? Master, give it day by day;
> Ever as the need arises, teach Thy children what to say.
> Give us holy love and patience; grant us deep humility,
> That of self we may be emptied, and our hearts be full of Thee;
> Give us zeal and faith and fervour, make us winning, make us wise,
> Single-hearted, strong and fearless;—Thou hast called us, we will rise!
> Let the might of Thy good Spirit go with every loving word;
> And by hearts prepared and opened, be our message always heard.

(My King)

That she had been given a 'ministry of song' was one of her strongest convictions. She believed that 'singing for Jesus' was the most personal and direct commission she had from her beloved Master, and though the opportunities for it were 'often most curious', they were greatly blessed.

NOT YOUR OWN

Teach us, Master, how to give
  All we have and are to Thee;
Grant us, Saviour while we live,
  Wholly, only, Thine to be.
Henceforth be our calling high
Thee to serve and glorify;
Ours no longer, but Thine own,
Thine for ever, Thine alone!

(last stanza; *The Ministry of Song*)

THE MINISTRY OF SONG

Sing on in grateful gladness!
  Rejoice in this good thing
Which the Lord thy God hath given thee,
  The happy power to sing.
But yield to Him, the Sovereign,
  To whom all gifts belong,
In fullest consecration,
  Your ministry of song.
Until His mercy grant you
  That resurrection voice,
Whose only ministry shall be,
  To praise Him and rejoice.

(last stanza; *The Ministry of Song*)

Chapter Four

Alpine Delight

'As the mountains are round about Jerusalem, so the Lord is
round about his people from henceforth even for ever.'
(Psalm 125:2)

OUR RED LETTER DAYS

My Alpine staff recalls each shining height,
    Each pass of grandeur with rejoicing gained,
    Carved with a lengthening record, self-explained,
Of mountain memories sublime and bright.
No valley-life but hath some mountain days,
    Bright summits in the retrospective view,
    And toil-worn passes to glad prospects new,
Fair sunlit memories of joy and praise.
Here then inscribe them,—each 'red letter day!'
Forget not all the sunshine of the way
By which the Lord hath led thee; answered prayers
And joys unasked, strange blessings, lifted cares,
Grand promise-echoes! Thus each page shall be
A record of God's love and faithfulness to thee!

(Red Letter Days)

From the letters sent to her home circle while Frances was
in Switzerland, it is evident that she had a great love for
mountains, and particularly the Alps. Her first sight of Mont Blanc
prompted the enthusiastic comment, 'Mountains, real ones, are more
to me than any other created being'.

Frances' visits to Switzerland took place between 1869-1876.
Usually her stay lasted six to eight weeks during the summer months,

and although she travelled extensively her preferences were for the Jungfrau, Matterhorn and Mont Blanc regions.

In these letters of her experiences she gives graphic descriptions, and they make very interesting reading. It seems that the Swiss air acted as salvolatile on her and, whereas at home she was not able to walk very far without tiring, among the mountains a five-hour climb was as nothing!

On her first trip in May 1869 Frances was accompanied by Henry Crane (H.C.), his wife (and Frances' sister) Miriam (M.) and their daughter Miriam Louisa (M.L.). They went via Dover and Calais, and making a stop over in Brussels she had her first opportunity to do what she loved best. A Belgian maid came into the hotel room where Frances was sitting and, after enquiring if she were comfortable, began telling her how ill she had been last year. Frances comments, 'That was a nice opportunity to speak of Him who "healeth all our diseases"'. The maid stayed talking for half an hour, saying she had an emptiness in her heart which was unsatisfied. After she had gone, Frances specially marked 'all I most wanted her to notice in a French St. John's Gospel and gave it to her next morning. She seemed pleased and promised to read it'. This was typical of Frances' desire to speak to people about the Saviour, and she always carried packs of literature with her to give away.

After travelling through several towns including Heidelberg and Basle, she and her companions stayed one night in Zurich and then travelled to Berne:

> Berne is quite the most novel and utterly foreign town I have seen: the streets arcaded like Chester, with bright red or orange cushions in every window seat, which touch up the grey stone effectively and complement the bright green venetian shutters. We ought to see the Alps from our windows at the Berner Hof [the hotel where they were staying]...but it is hopelessly misty.

It was here, though, soon after sunrise, that she had her first glimpse of the Alps:

> So now the dream of my life is realised, and I have seen snow mountains!...I always thought of eternal snow and perfect peace together, and longed to see the one and drink in the other. And I am not disappointed...I never saw anything material and earthly which so suggested the ethereal and heavenly, which so seemed to lead up to the unseen, to be the very steps of the Throne.

Travelling through the country, enjoying many great views of mountains and glaciers, they come to Pierre Pointue and Pierre A L'Echelle. Here Frances expresses her thoughts:

A real fine clear day at last! We inquired about the twinkle on the mountain and found it was the lamp at the little auberge at Pierre Pointue, the first stage up Mont Blanc; this was attractive so we went. A remarkably steep ride through the forest, and then far above it, brought us to Pierre Pointue in three hours. H.C.'s mules always go, though he does not appear to use any extra means, so he was there long before. M.L. and I have taken pains to acquire the mule language and its correct intonation; but all our Hu! Allez! Hupp! Carabi! Hui, hui! Allons! Arrrdi! is lost on them, and they pursue the even tenor of their way. Pierre Pointue commands a fine view of the Glacier des Bossons (a very fine one) and the snowy shoulder of Mont Blanc. We dismounted, and I had a real bona fide scramble an hour and a half higher up with H.C. and M.L. across the ends of snowdrifts, and right through torrents and up rocks and places you would not think feasible anywhere but in Switzerland. We rested and lunched with immense satisfaction...We were now about eight thousand six hundred feet high...It was marvellous how far up the lovely rhododendrons grow, but the forget-me-nots were almost as daring, and the Alpine ranunculus grew higher still, the special glacier flower, said Joseph Devouassoud [their guide]. It was a wild scene, the grim Rochers Rouges and Aiguille du Midi just above, the whole Dome du Goute shining close beyond the great glacier, an awful slope of snow and stones below us, and ever so deep down the Chamouni valley, which we must have seen as the birds see it.

She added the comment:

If there were any birds to see! But there is a curious paucity of them in Switzerland. We hardly ever saw or heard a bird of any kind. If we did, it was quite a thing to be remarked upon to each other. H.C. was always on the look out, he seemed to miss the birds and living creatures generally. Nature has devoted herself to the inanimate instead of the animate; one never sees a wild living thing except insects, which quite make up as regards numbers and beauty; no game, no rabbits, no nothing!

On a summit above the Col de Balm, 'which commands one of the most sublime and perfect panoramas in the world', she comments:

A regular carpet of flowers, chiefly forget-me-nots, gentianellas, brilliant potentillas, violets, pansies and daises, and many lovely flowers

I did not know. The grasses too were various and pretty. What an addition to the enjoyment of the great, the small can be! And there I wrote these lines:

THE COL DE BALM

SUNSHINE and Silence on the Col de Balm!
I stood above the mists, above the rush
Of all the torrents, when one marvellous hush
Filled God's great mountain temple, vast and calm,
With hallelujah light, a seen though silent psalm.

(first stanza; *Under the Surface*)

On their way to Chamouni, she asked a guide, Aristide Couttet, to tell her the rules and arrangements about guides, which he apparently explained clearly and intelligently. 'But do not visitors sometimes go to the mountains without a guide?' He answered just what she wanted him to say! 'Oh, yes, madame but it is very foolish; they only lose their way, and it is very dangerous. Accidents happen when they will go without one, but if one has a guide all goes well'. 'We have a Guide, Aristide; do you know who I mean?' 'Oh, yes madame; you mean Jesus Christ, He is the best guide…One does not fear death if one has that Guide' he said; 'He gives us salvation'. She gave him some little Scripture papers and after he had glanced over them, he put his finger on some verses about the Saviour (John 3:16 was one), and said, 'C'est bien joli, cela' ["This is good, very good"].

Having arrived in Interlaken, they went to the highest hotel in the town and from there Frances writes:

Here we are perched on a terrace looking down into the valley, with the Jungfrau looking down upon us between two steep wooded hills, shining out of grey clouds every now and then like a sudden smile, with that wonderful intensity of whiteness which to me gives a totally new force to "whiter than snow". And I see too how perfectly the evangelists complete each other's description of our Lord's transfiguration raiment (St. Matthew says it was "white as the light"; St. Mark "exceeding white as snow") for this Alpine snow is light materialised and snow etherealised, it is a combination of the impressions of each.

From Interlaken they set off for Lauterbrunnen:

Fancy nine miles' drive up a deep valley, hills six or seven thousand feet high on each side, wooded wherever trees could get root, and where not, rocky and precipitous, between them at each opening views of snow mountains glittering in brilliant light; below, a wild stream, the Lutschine, rushing in one perpetual downhill of rapids and little falls; every now and then a silver thread of a waterfall gleaming out on the farther side of the valley, or a broad riband of one dashing down the nearer side to our very feet, to be crossed by a little bridge, then the whole picture "grounded" with shades of the freshest, brightest green, still wet with the morning's rain and canopied with vivid blue. And at every turn coming nearer to the Jungfrau, "Queen of the Alps", which fills up the valley in front, and only hides herself again when we get too close under her silver throne.

It struck me again here, as in Scotland last summer, what marvellous lavishment of beauty God has poured upon the details of His works. For here, in the presence of these culminations of earthly magnificence, scenes beyond what we ever saw before, if the eye dropped and rested on the very ground it was just as beautiful in its proportion as if there were no other loveliness for us far or near; ferns and flowers and grasses, and mossy boulders, and tiny streams, every square foot being a little world of beauty.

On the way to Grindelwald, Frances had plenty of opportunity to give out tracts and Bible portions. Their driver was given a copy of Luke's Gospel and the next evening he showed it to Frances and said it was a treasure that he would never part with.

He had got it out at supper, and read it to the roomful of guides and drivers; most of them approved, and two or three wanted to buy it from him, but he said he would not give it up for anything. Then he read some more aloud, whereupon a godless guide began scoffing and blaspheming; not ten minutes after, he cut his hand, or rather wrist, so fearfully that he was quite ill, and the driver said they thought that he would be laid up for a fortnight, the loss of blood being so great as to be dangerous;...The others were quite impressed, and said it was a judgment of God upon him. This old driver seemed to have the fear of God, and listened earnestly and responded warmly to all I tried to tell him.

At Vevey, Henry Crane and Frances rowed seven miles across Lake Geneva to St. Gingolph, and then walked up the Gorge de la Morge. After a three-hour uphill trek to a village 8000 ft. above the lake they halted at an inn for refreshments, and being now footsore they asked their host if there was any alternative means of descent.

His reply was 'sanguine but mysterious'; all would be well but they must wait. Eventually their host arrived with his 'beautiful new carriage' and its 'horse'—himself!

This is how Frances describes their unusual conveyance:

> Its foundation was a hay sledge, two little wheels behind with two thick runners, joined by rough crossbars. On this our host had tied with ropes an old wine chest; across it was a plank with a manifest bolster on it as a cushion. Two long crooked sticks were tied to the runners for shafts. 'Montez, monsieur, we will go like the chemin de fer, vous verrez!' so in we got...He waved his cap to his wife, with whom he was evidently on the best of terms, and set off full tear, downhill. It was no use shouting 'Doucement!' He only looked round and laughed, and tugged away at the shafts, over boulders and holes, and swinging round corners on the very edge of the deep gully, till really if we had not been incapacitated by laughing from either thinking or doing anything else, we should have been seriously frightened.

While their 'horse' proceeded at breakneck speed, Frances and Henry gave their attention to hanging on and trying to balance the machine. Let Frances relate the end of the journey:

> About a quarter of a mile from the bottom, just as we were getting used to the said balancing, and our steed getting more careless, we were swung round a corner and over some unexpectedly large stones, when suddenly we felt a most queer giving-way earthquaky sensation, and roared to a halt simultaneously. Just as the man contrived to stop, the whole concern came bodily to grief, all to pieces at once in a most surprising style, cords yielded, shafts broke, nails came out, and boards subsided into one shapeless heap, from which we extricated ourselves with nothing more than a bruise or two, laughing more than ever, for it made the thing so very complete to have such a proper and thorough breakdown, it was the only finishing touch it wanted.

Needless to say, they finished their journey on foot.

In June of 1871 Frances and her close friend Elizabeth Clay spent some weeks in Switzerland. Frances mentioned travelling from Newhaven to Rouen via Dieppe. Her friend had brought a stock of little French books and tracts which they divided between them and soon started to put them to good use.

> We gave many away, and you cannot think how delighted people seemed. One tall grave man, of superior rank, watched us, and came up to E. asking if she had many. We were afraid he meant to interfere,

as he looked very official; however, he only wanted to ask 'if we would kindly give him one for himself, two if we could'. He took them, and thanked us as if we had given him some great thing.

Frances mentions their stay in the Hotel Mont Blanc just outside Courmayeur and comments:

The hours here are most original. We are supposed to have coffee early, when we like, then at 10 a.m. a dejeuner table d'hote; this was, first a white grainy compound with grated cheese supposed to be soup, then sliced German sausage and bread and butter, then very good cutlets and fried potatoes, then stewed pears, then cheese, then apricots, etc. The second table d'hote is at five. There are about thirty-two Italians and Piedmontese in the house; no English; they are rather noisy, but very amusing to watch. After breakfast we strayed into the salon de lecture, and found a tolerable piano, the first we have had; so naturally I sat down, there being only two ladies in the room, played a bit, and finally sang. I was rather startled after the latter performance to hear a vehement round of clapping. I had no idea of it, but the room had filled quietly; I had my back to them, and found I had a room full of Italians as audience, quite a new thing for me! And they seemed amazingly pleased. Actually the waiters brought more chairs in, seeing the concourse, to my great amusement; so what could I do but yield to the requests, and sing two more songs! We are not the least tired as yet, but mean to have three hours' siesta; we always make up our short nights.

Walking up the Reuss valley, Frances writes from Geschenen: 'Hurrah! We are in a most exhilarated state of mind, just like children; and, except a little undercurrent of general thanksgiving we don't feel solemn at all, and have been in the wildest spirits.'

On another occasion, when Frances was out for a walk, she came across an old woman knitting and tending goats in a 'lovely dingle'; Frances sat down by her and read out of the German Testament which she carried with her. Apparently the old woman was delighted and Frances had an interesting talk with her.

One of her favourite guides was Joseph Devouassoud and on one occasion he asked her to write a testimonial in his book. She wrote without hesitation:

Careful and gentle, respectful and steady,
Always obliging and watchful and ready;
Pleasantly telling, as children say,
All about everything on the way;

Good for the glaciers, strong for the steeps;
Mighty for mountains, and lithesome for leaps;
Guide of experience, trusty and true,
None can be better than Devouassoud!

(*Swiss Letters and Alpine Poems*)

She gave him a free translation which seemed to please him greatly.

It was while Frances was at the hotel in Zermatt that she discovered hay duvets. These consisted of a large doubled square of coloured print, neat and clean, lightly filled with loose hay. She thought it was an excellent idea and one to be put into practice when she visited the poor people back at home; it would cost little money or effort yet would be so welcome and add a little comfort to their hard lot.

On a particular day, the two intrepid travellers were set to climb the Sparrenhorn which is nearly 10,000 feet high. They had secured one of the best guides for this trip—Anton Walden—and set off just after 3:30 a.m.

Now I have seen it at last, a real Alpine dawn and sunrise to perfection! We saw the 'daffodil sky'…in the east, a calm glory of expectant light, as if something positively celestial must come next, instead of merely the usual sun. In the south-west the grandest mountains stood white and perfectly clear, as if they might be waiting for the resurrection.

When they were on their way down with their guide, Anton Walden, Frances enjoyed two glissades, one on her own and the other with the guide. 'It was such fun, he caught his foot and was all but down, and I held him up; he laughed no end at this, and gave me full credit for it'. She was pleased to be able to have 'some little talks' with Anton who told her that it was not acceptable for his people to read the New Testament for themselves; 'but there are a few free spirits among us who read notwithstanding'. She spoke to him about asking the Holy Spirit to teach him whenever he read the Testament (which is all he had), and he replied that that was just what he thought too; he had found that out of his New Testament, and had prayed for the Holy Spirit.

Frances always spoke of this holiday as the most enjoyable of all her Swiss tours, and as the two travellers bade farewell to the Alps the words came to her:

The works of the Lord are great,
sought out of all them that have pleasure therein.
(Psalm 111:2)

In the summer of 1873 Frances accompanied her friends, the Rev. and Mrs. Charles B. Snepp, and their daughter, Emily, to Switzerland. In spite of Mr. Snepp's age, he was to prove no less adventurous than Frances herself. Whilst on one of their climbing expeditions it was Mr. Snepp who came to the rescue when Frances could have had a serious, even fatal, accident but for his intervention. The guide had insisted on their being roped—the guides, then Frances, then Mr. S. last, saying this was the safest arrangement. All but Frances had leather belts with a metal ring like a harness. This was too heavy for Frances, so she was simply noosed round the waist with a firm knot. About eight or ten feet of rope were allowed between each person. Although Frances preferred not to be roped so as to have more freedom to glissade, she was thankful that she had been on this occasion:

> I thought we were come to a sufficiently easy part to go carelessly, whereupon I slipped, and Payot [the guide] who was next me totally lost himself too, and we had just started a decidedly too rapid spin down a very steep incline, when instantaneously Mr. S. did the only possible thing which could have stopped all four of us; flung himself right on his back with his heels in the snow, the orthodox thing to do if only any one has the presence of mind to do it. This checked the impetus, and we quickly recovered our footing.

All of this about Frances' mountaineering is quite pertinent to her writing. In choosing analogies to express spiritual truths Frances rarely went beyond the language of Scripture. She does, however, occasionally use imagery derived from mountaineering, and this in itself is evidence of what the experience must have meant to her. A favourite analogy is that of the Swiss guide. Her own adventures on the mountains gave her an insight into the character of these remarkable men, and as she meditated on times when her own foolhardiness had nearly brought disaster, and other times when absolute obedience to the guide had been the secret of safe and successful climbing, she saw in her own relationship with the guides an analogy of the Christian's relationship to Christ.

One detail of the guide's equipment which intrigued her was the Alpine Club rope:

> Once I questioned the strength of the rope, upon which the guide untwisted it a little, and showed me a scarlet thread hidden among the strands. He told me that this was the mark that it was a real Alpine Club rope, manufactured expressly for that purpose, and to be depended upon in a matter of life and death. It is remarkable that this typical 'line of scarlet thread' should have been selected as the guarantee of safety.

With Frances' knowledge of the Scriptures it was not surprising that she linked this rope with the scarlet cord hanging from Rahab's window, guaranteeing the safety of her household when Jericho was attacked, and drew the analogy that Christ was Saviour and Guide to all who are united to Him 'by the strong cords of His eternal purpose and His everlasting love'.

Frances' last visit to Switzerland was in July 1876 in company with her sister Maria. While they were in Champery, they met Baroness Helga von Cramm, who was to become a very dear friend to Frances. She loved painting and her two specialities were Alpine flowers and Alpine scenery. She produced some remarkable paintings which illustrated several of Frances' published books.

THE PENSION WENGEN

Towards the end of this visit Frances became very ill; she and Maria were staying at the Pension Wengen above Lauterbrunnen, and on Sunday afternoon, October 8, while seeking to bear the pain with patient submission, she wrote:

A SONG IN THE NIGHT

I take this pain, Lord Jesus,
From Thine own hand,
The strength to bear it bravely
Thou wilt command.

'Tis Thy dear hand, O Saviour,
That presseth sore,
The hand that bears the nail-prints
For evermore.

(first and eleventh stanzas; *Under His Shadow*)

It was not until late October that she was well enough to travel home. On the homeward journey inspiration was given for writing her little book *My King,* and although illness came on again, the book was quickly finished and published.

Through these *Swiss Letters* and *Alpine Poems* we have been given an insight into Frances' character; though her life for the most part was marked by seriousness, we have glimpsed those times when her humour shone through. She was often smiling, laughing and causing others to laugh. We have also seen how much she appreciated the beauty of God's creation, animate and inanimate, and how she took every opportunity to speak for her Master.

THE MOUNTAIN MAIDENS

Father who hast made the mountains,
Who hast formed each tiny flower,
Who hast filled the crystal fountains,
Who hast sent us sun and shower.
Hear Thy children's morning prayer,
Asking for Thy guardian care;
Keep and guide us all the day,
Lead us safely all the way.

(first stanza of the Chorale; *Swiss Letters and Alpine Poems*)

1. This was one of eight photographs taken by Elliott and Fry in London, in February 1879, a few months before Frances' unanticipated early death.

2. This chalk portrait by T. J. Hughes was made in Frances' last year, when she was 42. Although it is thought that this is not a flattering portrait of her, it is considered to be an accurate one.

From a Painting
by S. Cole.

3. William Henry Havergal (1793-1870). This print is based on a colour portrait by
Solomon Cole, likely painted in 1845.

Map do ṡráḋṁ an ċuṡam ṁṁṡ, aṫ map ṁ do ṡráḋṁ ṁṁṡ ḃḃṡ.

• • • • • • • • • • • • • • • •

4. This harp—which was Frances' personal emblem—was hand painted in an autograph album she had. The Irish shamrocks and all the artwork were painted in gold by an unknown friend. The statement below the harp is written in modern Irish but using an old form of Irish lettering, and is the first part of John 15:9: 'As the Father hath loved Me, so have I loved you'.

5. Frances' manuscript score "Whom having not seen, ye love."

THE

MINISTRY OF SONG.

BY

FRANCES RIDLEY HAVERGAL.

SECOND EDITION.

LONDON:

CHRISTIAN BOOK SOCIETY,

22 KING WILLIAM STREET, STRAND.

. . . .

6. This is the title page of Frances' first published book, in an early copy by the London Christian Book Society, before James Nisbet & Co. became her publisher.

SONGS

OF

GRACE AND GLORY.

NEW AND ENLARGED

MUSICAL EDITION.

𝕳𝔂𝔪𝔫𝔞𝔩 𝔞𝔫𝔡 𝔐𝔲𝔰𝔦𝔠𝔞𝔩 𝔗𝔯𝔢𝔞𝔰𝔲𝔯𝔢𝔰 𝔬𝔣 𝔱𝔥𝔢 𝔆𝔥𝔲𝔯𝔠𝔥 𝔬𝔣 𝔆𝔥𝔯𝔦𝔰𝔱

FROM MANY CENTURIES.

EDITED BY THE LATE

FRANCES RIDLEY HAVERGAL,

AND

CHARLES B. SNEPP, LL.M.,

Vicar of Perry Barr.

FULL EDITION OF 1100 HYMNS WITH TUNES.

LONDON: JAMES NISBET AND CO., 21, BERNERS STREET.

MDCCCLXXX.

. . . .

7. *Songs of Grace and Glory* was a labour of love, in which she prepared the music for 1,100 hymns. She began this work in 1870, and after a number of editions, she finalized the scores for this definitive edition in her last year, 1879.

"Whose I am, and

Jesus, Master, whose I am
    Purchased Thine alone to be
By thy blood, O spotless Lamb,
    Shed so willingly for me;
Let my heart be all thine own,
Let me live to Thee alone.

Other lords have long held sway,
    Now, Thy name alone to bear,
Thy dear voice alone obey,
    Is my daily, hourly prayer.
Whom have I in heaven but Thee?
Nothing else my joy can be.

Jesus, Master! I am Thine;
    Keep me faithful, keep me near;
Let thy presence in me shine
    All my homeward way to cheer.
Jesus! at thy feet I fall,
Oh, be Thou my All in all!

. . . .

8. This and the adjoining facing page are Frances Ridley Havergal's fair copy autographs
of two of her poems, in a Manuscript Book she kept for poems. Frances changed the

"Whom I serve". Acts 27. 23.

Jesus, Master! whom I serve,
  Though so feebly & so ill,
Strengthen hand & heart & nerve
  All Thy bidding to fulfil.
Open Thou mine eyes to see
All the work Thou hast for me.

Lord! Thou needest not, I know,
  Service such as I can bring;
Yet I long to prove & show
  Full allegiance to my King.
Thou an* honour art to me,
Let me be a praise to Thee.

Jesus, Master! wilt Thou use
  One who owes Thee more than all?
As Thou wilt! I would not choose,
  Only let me hear thy call.
Jesus! let me always be
In thy service glad and free.

Dec. 1865.

* See marginal
reading of I Pet. 2. 7.

30

. . . .

second to fourth lines of the second stanza. She published these in her first book, *The Ministry of Song*, in 1869.

"Yea, let him take all!"

Take my life, and let it be
Consecrated, Lord, to Thee.

Take my hands, and let them move
With the impulse of thy love.

Take my feet, & let them be
Swift & beautiful for Thee.

Take my voice and let me sing
Always, only, for my King.

Take my lips, & let them be
Filled with messages from Thee,

Take my silver & my gold,
Not a mite would I withhold

. . . .

9. This and the adjoining facing page are Frances' fair copy autograph of the 'Consecration Hymn', written in her Manuscript Book soon after the hymn's original

Take my moments & my days,
Let them flow in ceaseless praise.

Take my intellect, & use
Every power as thou dost choose

Take my will & make it Thine
It shall be no longer mine

Take my heart! it is Thine own!
It shall be Thy royal throne!

Take my love, my Lord I pour
At Thy feet its treasure-store

Take myself & I will be
Ever, Only, All, for Thee!

Fleur. Sal. R. Leaflets.
Golden Grain. W.VW. S.C.C.
B͞u, Oxf. & N. hymnbooks.

Feb. 4.

. . . .

conception. There are a number of differences between this early copy and the finalized text that she published as Day One of her fifth Royal Book, *Loyal Responses*, the
finalized text that we know today.

10. On this and the adjoining facing page is a list of work that was found in Frances Ridley Havergal's desk after her death. A number of these were either left unfinished or never begun.

X Select or write "Echoes from the Word" for Day of Days.

X Sets of New Year's Mottoes for Caswell v— ~~Five~~ sets of six.

Bright Thoughts for Dark Days. (set for Caswell.)

Series of Irish Sketches for D. of D

Sunday Postal Burdens — mag. paper

~~Our Brother; or Daily Thoughts for those who love~~

Our Brother; or Daily Thoughts for those who love Him

X Morning Stars; or Daily Thoughts about Jesus for the little ones

Evening Stars; or Promises for the little ones.

Complete the series of Sunday morning Crumbs.

Six Poems for Sunday Magazine.

SABBATH SCHOOL

11. These are two pages from Frances Ridley Havergal's Worcester Sunday School register.

CLASS REGISTER.

MONTH OF 18	MONTH OF 18	MONTH OF 18	MONTH OF 18	
SABBATHS	SABBATHS	SABBATHS	SABBATHS	

<table>
<tr><td>29</td><td>5 12 17</td><td></td><td></td><td></td><td></td><td></td></tr>
<tr><td>X</td><td></td><td></td><td></td><td></td><td></td><td></td></tr>
<tr><td>X</td><td></td><td></td><td></td><td>1.</td><td>I Kings</td><td>10. 1-13</td></tr>
<tr><td>X</td><td></td><td></td><td></td><td>2</td><td>I Sam</td><td>22. 9, 23</td></tr>
<tr><td>X</td><td></td><td></td><td></td><td></td><td>I Chr.</td><td>12. 18.</td></tr>
<tr><td>X</td><td></td><td></td><td></td><td>3</td><td>I Sam</td><td>25. 32-41.</td></tr>
<tr><td>X</td><td></td><td></td><td></td><td>4</td><td>Cant 1.</td><td>1 - 4.</td></tr>
<tr><td>X</td><td></td><td></td><td></td><td>5</td><td>Cant 1.</td><td>4, 5.</td></tr>
<tr><td>X</td><td></td><td></td><td></td><td>6</td><td>Cant 1.</td><td>6 - 8.</td></tr>
<tr><td>X</td><td></td><td></td><td></td><td>7</td><td>Num.</td><td>35. 9 - 34</td></tr>
<tr><td>X</td><td></td><td></td><td></td><td></td><td></td><td></td></tr>
<tr><td>—</td><td></td><td></td><td></td><td></td><td></td><td></td></tr>
<tr><td></td><td></td><td>s</td><td>Fanny Bayliss</td><td>X X</td><td></td><td></td></tr>
<tr><td>X</td><td></td><td></td><td>Edith Palmer</td><td>X X</td><td></td><td></td></tr>
<tr><td>X</td><td></td><td>s</td><td>Hannah Bury</td><td>X X</td><td></td><td></td></tr>
<tr><td>X</td><td></td><td>s</td><td>Mary Coclus</td><td>X -</td><td></td><td></td></tr>
<tr><td>X</td><td></td><td></td><td>Emma Elcox</td><td>X X</td><td></td><td></td></tr>
<tr><td>X</td><td></td><td></td><td>Foster</td><td>X X</td><td></td><td></td></tr>
<tr><td>—</td><td></td><td></td><td></td><td></td><td></td><td></td></tr>
<tr><td>gone</td><td></td><td></td><td></td><td></td><td></td><td></td></tr>
<tr><td>X</td><td></td><td></td><td>H. Bury</td><td>X</td><td></td><td></td></tr>
<tr><td>X</td><td></td><td></td><td>Emily Foster</td><td>X</td><td></td><td></td></tr>
<tr><td>—</td><td></td><td></td><td></td><td></td><td></td><td></td></tr>
<tr><td>—</td><td></td><td></td><td></td><td></td><td></td><td></td></tr>
<tr><td>24</td><td></td><td></td><td></td><td></td><td></td><td></td></tr>
</table>

31 I have stuck unto thy testimonies : O LORD, put me not to*a* shame.

32 I will run the way of thy commandments, when thou shalt enlarge*b* my heart.
HE.

33 Teach me, O LORD, the way of thy statutes, and I shall keep*d* it *unto* the end.

34 Give*e* me understanding, and*f* I shall keep thy law; yea, I shall observe it with *my* whole heart.

35 Make me to go in the path of thy commandments; for therein do I delight.

36 Incline my heart*i* unto thy testimonies, and not to*k* covetousness.

37 β Turn away mine eyes from beholding*l* vanity; *and* quicken thou me in thy way.

38 Stablish*m* thy word unto thy servant, who *is devoted* to thy fear.

39 Turn away my reproach which I fear: for thy judgments *are* good.

40 Behold, I have longed after thy precepts: quicken*p* me in thy righteousness.
VAU.

41 Let thy mercies come also unto me, O LORD; *even* thy salvation, according to thy word.

42 So shall I γhave wherewith to answer him that reproacheth me: for I trust in thy word.

43 And take not*e* the word of truth utterly out of my mouth; for I have hoped in thy judgments.

44 So shall I keep thy law continually for ever and ever.

45 And I will walk at η liberty:*u* for I seek thy precepts.

46 I will speak of thy testimonies also before kings,*w* and will not be ashamed.

47 And I will delight myself in thy commandments, which I have loved.

48 My hands also will I lift up unto thy commandments, which I have loved; and I will meditate in thy statutes.
ZAIN.

49 Remember the word unto thy servant, upon which thou hast caused me to*a* hope.

50 This *is* my comfort in my affliction: for thy word hath quickened me.

51 The proud have had me greatly in derision; *yet*b have I not declined from thy law.

52 I remembered thy judgments of old, O LORD; and have comforted myself.

53 Horror*c* hath taken hold upon me, because of the wicked that forsake thy law.

54 Thy statutes have been my songs in the house of my pilgrimage.

55 I have remembered thy name, O LORD, in the night,*g* and have kept thy law.

56 This I had, because I kept thy precepts.
CHETH.

57 Thou art my portion,*h* O LORD: I have said that I would keep thy words.

58 I entreated thy κfavour with *my* whole*k* heart: be merciful unto me according to thy word.

59 I thought*l* on my ways, and turned my feet unto thy testimonies.

60 I made haste, and delayed not, to keep thy commandments.

61 The *v*bands of the wicked have robbed me: *but* I have not forgotten thy law.

62 At midnight I will rise to give thanks unto thee, because of thy righteous judgments.

63 I *am* a companion*o* of all *them* that fear thee, and of them that keep thy precepts.

64 The earth, O LORD, is full of thy mercy: teach me thy statutes.

a Is. 49. 23.
b Is. 60. 5.
2 Co. 6. 11.
c Je. 3. 15.
d Re. 2. 26.
e Pr. 2. 6.
f De. 4. 6.
g Je.31.18,19.
He. 12. 11.
h Ps. 25. 8.
Mat. 19. 17.
i Eze. 33. 31.
k Lu. 12. 15.
1 Ti. 6. 10.
He. 13. 5.
β *Make to pass.*
l Is. 33. 15.
m 2 Sa. 7. 25.
2 Co. 1. 20.
n verse 67.
o Ps. 19. 10.
Pr.8.11,19.
p John 10. 10.
q ver. 34,144.
Ps. 111. 10.
r Ps. 34. 2.
γ or, *answer him that reproacheth me in a thing.*
δ *righteousness.*
s Is. 59. 21.
t Re. 3. 19.
ζ *to comfort me.*
η *large.*
u Jno.8.32,36
Ga. 5. 1, 13.
v 1 Pe. 2. 20.
w Mat. 10. 18, 19.
Ac. 26.1,&c.
x De. 26. 16.
Eze. 11. 19.
y verse 6.
z Ps. 84. 2.
a 1 Pe.1.13,21
b Job 23. 11.
c 2 Th. 1. 9.
Re. 6. 10.
d Ps. 35. 7.
e Ezr. 9. 3.
f verse 138.
θ *faithfulness.*
g Ps. 63. 6.
77. 6.
h Je. 10. 16.
La. 3. 24.
i Mat. 24. 34, 35.
κ *face,*
Job 11. 19.
λ *to generation and generation,*
Ps. 89. 1.
k He. 10. 22.
μ *standeth.*
l La.3.40,41.
Lu.15.17,18
m Je. 33. 25.
ν or, *companies.*
n Zep. 3. 17.
o Pr. 13. 20.

Jos 23.14. *P.* 13.6
P. 126. 9; 142. 7.   **TETH.**   *Joel* 2.26.

65 Thou hast dealt well with thy servant, O LORD, according unto thy word.

66 Teach*c* me good judgment and knowledge: for I have believed thy commandments.

67 Before I was afflicted*g* I went astray; but now have I kept thy word.

68 Thou*h art* good, and doest good: teach me thy statutes.

69 The proud have forged a lie against me: *but* I will keep thy precepts with *my* whole heart.

70 Their heart is as fat as grease: *but* I delight in thy law.

71 *It*n *is* good for me that I have been afflicted; that I might learn thy statutes.

72 The*o* law of thy mouth *is* better unto me than thousands of gold and silver.
JOD.

73 Thy hands have made me, and fashioned me: give me understanding, that I may learn thy commandments.

74 They*r* that fear thee will be glad when they see me; because I have hoped in thy word.

75 I know, O LORD, that thy judgments *are* δright, and *that* thou in faithfulness*t* hast afflicted me.

76 Let, I pray thee, thy merciful kindness be ζfor my comfort, according to thy word unto thy servant.

77 Let thy tender mercies come unto me, that I may live: for thy law *is* my delight.

78 Let the proud be ashamed; for they dealt perversely with me without*u* a cause: *but* I will meditate in thy precepts.

79 Let those that fear thee turn unto me, and those that have known thy testimonies.

80 Let my heart be sound*x* in thy statutes, that I be not*y* ashamed.
CAPH.

81 My soul fainteth*z* for thy salvation; *but* I hope in thy word.

82 Mine eyes fail for thy word, saying, When wilt thou comfort me?

83 For I am become like a bottle in the smoke; *yet* do I not forget thy statutes.

84 How many *are* the days of thy servant? when*c* wilt thou execute judgment on them that persecute me?

85 The proud have digged*d* pits for me, which *are* not after thy law.

86 All*f* thy commandments *are* θfaithful: they persecute me wrongfully; help thou me.

87 They had almost consumed me upon earth: but I forsook not thy precepts.

88 Quicken me after thy lovingkindness; so shall I keep the testimony of thy mouth.
LAMED.

89 For*i* ever, O LORD, thy word is settled in heaven.

90 Thy faithfulness *is* λunto all generations; thou hast established the earth, and it μ abideth.

91 They continue this day according to thine ordinances:*m* for all *are* thy servants.

92 Unless thy law *had been* my delights, I should then have perished in mine affliction.

93 I will never forget thy precepts: for with them thou hast quickened me.

94 I *am* thine, save*n* me: for I have sought thy precepts.

95 The wicked have waited for me, to destroy me: *but* I will consider thy testimonies.

96 I have seen an end of all perfection: *but* thy commandment *is* exceeding broad.

399

· · · · · · · · · · · · · · · ·

12. This is a page from Frances' last study Bible, a Bagster Bible that she was using at the end of her life.

16. Worcester Cathedral, where Frances made a public profession of faith in Christ at her Confirmation when she was 17. Frances was living near the River Severn when she wrote the hymn on Isaiah 26:3, *"Like a river glorious is God's perfect peace."*

17. The River Severn. Photo Courtesy of John Mountford, Birmingham, U.K.

18. This plaque was placed on a stone wall at the house in 1937. "To the Glory of God and in ever loving remembrance of Frances Ridley Havergal Christian poetess and hymnwriter who lived at this house and died here on 3rd June 1879. 'She, being dead, yet speaketh.' Erected by public subscription July, 1937." Photo Courtesy of Mr. David Haslam.

19. This is the house in Mumbles where Frances lived her last eight months and died on June 3, 1879. Photo Courtesy of Mrs C. Webbern.

Chapter Five

The Five Royal Books

A railway carriage may seem an unlikely place to have inspiration for writing a book, but so it was with Frances. Her last visit to Switzerland in June 1876 ended in severe illness, and her return home had to be delayed until late October. Let Maria recall what happened:

> It was October 21st, we had passed Oxford station, on our way to Winterdyne, and I thought she was dozing, when she suddenly exclaimed, with that herald flash in her eye, 'Marie! I see it all, I can write a little book *My King*', and rapidly went through divisions for thirty one chapters.

Although illness and severe suffering came on again soon afterwards, the book was quickly written and published. The purpose of these *Royal Books* was to give a meditation or poem for each day of the month.

On the First Day of *My King or Daily Thoughts for the King's Children* she wrote:

> So the source of the Kingship of Christ is God Himself in the eternal counsels of His love…Having provided, He appointed and anointed His King. The sections of this book are taken from Old Testament texts. Why has God made Jesus King? Because the Lord loved His people. He knows our need of a King.

On the Thirtieth Day of this book Frances quotes 2 Kings 7:9, commenting on the story of the four lepers. C.H. Spurgeon used this in a sermon entitled 'Public Testimony: A Debt to God and Man'. While talking about bearing witness to make Christ known he commented, 'I wish that we did this more often amongst God's own people'. He goes on to say: "Miss Havergal very admirably says, 'The King's household were the most unlikely people to need to be instructed in this good news; so it seems at first sight. But secondly the lepers were the most unlikely persons to instruct the King's household; and yet they did so'". He points out that Christians should be concerned to talk about their faith to one another as much as to unbelievers, but for one reason or another "perhaps you begin talking upon worthless themes: you speak of the weather, or of the last wretched scandal, or of politics. Suppose we were to change all this, and each one say, '... next time I meet a brother Christian, whether he is my superior or not, I shall speak to him of our common Master'".

Another interesting link we have is a comment from J.P. Hobson related in the book *Excellent Women* (published by the London Tract Society in the 1880s):

> The writer [Hobson]...may here refer to a never-to-be-forgotten hour that he spent with Frances R. Havergal. He had sent her some lines suggested by this little book, of which she most kindly expressed her approval, and naturally the book *My King* formed the subject of conversation, and she expressed her gratitude that she had been led to write this and other of her books in chapters for each day in the month; 'for', said she, 'they are read through in many cases twelve times a year instead of being perused once and thrown aside'.

Writing to a friend she commented:

> *My King* has been the greatest writing pleasure I ever had! And in it I have said my say about lots of little points on which I wanted to have a say, and *My King* seemed to indicate a nice opportunity in this form... The title...is in itself a very song of joy to me...I am afraid you will smile at some sentences in it, but I do not seem able to help saying absurd things in prose, especially when I want to hit a nail hard and square on the head!

Mr. S.G. Prout was a friend she had a lot to do with in connexion with a book he wrote entitled *Never Say Die*. He evidently said he had enjoyed her book *My King* to which Frances made the interesting response:

Perhaps you would hardly guess how very much what you said about *My King* delighted and encouraged me. I never expected men to read or care for it—I did not aim higher than girls of whom I have a considerable following. It is far more than I hoped—for I am not one of those terrible 'strong-minded women', but I think we have quite 'rights' enough in proportion to our powers and position. And I never thought of reaching men by anything I might write; yet you and others are willing to listen to the little things I have to say, and I take it as an extra token for good—the more pleasant, because unsought and unexpected.

Her sister Maria tells two of her nephews that she had many letters after the death of their aunt, speaking of blessing received from her writings, 'A Unitarian wrote to her, that since reading *My King*, he has left his false doctrines and loves the Lord Jesus.'

Frances wrote five *Royal Books* altogether, each with a distinctive purpose. The others are:

Royal Commandments or Morning Thoughts for the King's Servants

Some of His Royal Commandments are made so 'plain upon tables, that he may run that readeth'...Some are engraved upon the gems of promise, and as we look closely into the fair colours of each jewel that the hand of faith receives, we find that it is enriched by an unerasable line of precept. But all are royal, and all are 'from Him', our King. And He has said, 'If ye love Me, keep My commandments'.

A quote from the Thirtieth Day of this book is:

'This do in remembrance of Me':...Luther said: 'I feel as if Jesus Christ died yesterday'. So fresh, so vivid, be our love and thankfulness! But may we add: 'And as if He were coming today'. Then our lives would indeed be rich in remembrance and radiant in anticipation.

Royal Bounty or Evening Thoughts for the King's Guests

'The Lord shall open unto thee His good treasure'. This book describes the gracious provision of our King to His subjects, the benefits of the Christian life, the unsearchable riches of Christ in Whom are hidden all the treasures of wisdom and knowledge. 'Faith is the key to this infinite treasury'.

On the Seventh Day of this book she writes:

> He loveth at all times, and that includes the present moment; now, while your eye is on this page, His eye is looking on you, and the folds of His banner of love are overshadowing you.

Loyal Responses or Daily Melodies for the King's Minstrels

> These are 31 poems, in which almost every line has been either directly drawn from Holy Scripture or 'may be proved thereby'. May not only our lips but our lives be filled with Loyal Responses to all the words of our King!

In the *Treasury of David*, in his exposition of Psalm 121, C. H. Spurgeon quoted the second stanza of F.R.H.'s poem 'Looking unto Jesus' (in the Thirteenth Day of this book):

> Look away to Jesus!
>   Look away from all;
> Then we need not stumble,
>   Then we shall not fall.
> From each snare that lureth
>   Foe or phantom grim,
> Safety this ensureth:
>   Look away to Him.

The Royal Invitation or Daily Thoughts on Coming to Christ

> The human heart within us craves a personal, living rest and refuge...The great word of Invitation, Royal and Divine, is given to us, 'Come unto Me'. This is the Son of God, mighty to save and ready to save all who come unto Him. In Him are life and peace.

This was the last of the *Royal Books* to be written, and in January 1878 Frances writes to a friend:

> I meant to have set to work this morning at my new book, *The Royal Invitation*, but instead of that, I give the time to prayer, and requests for prayer about it. Tomorrow I hope to begin...I must write it—I must set aside other things for it, and yet, most strangely, I have not two ideas as to what to say! All I know is that...the keynote must be 'COME'.
>
> You see, I have only written for Christians as yet...and so I have not fulfilled the great commission, 'Let him that heareth say, Come' in writing, though of course I am often at it in speaking. So now I want to peal out a COME that shall be heard and followed; a 'Come' especially

to those who are not reached by tracts or little books in paper covers, but who would not reject a pretty gift-book of daily readings, not too long and not too prosy.

It will want special tact and power, and all that I have not got, and must therefore look only to the Lord for! The other books have opened a wide door for it; and if I am enabled to do it at all, it will probably go by tens of thousands, and so it is an immense responsibility to dare to write it. I feel as if it were hardly less than preaching to one of Moody's enormous congregations!

Now won't you and your good friends help me mightily about it? Ask that He would give me EVERY SINGLE WORD from beginning to end...please ask that it may be FULL OF POWER—that every chapter may be a channel of converting grace.

There! Have I asked too much? I don't mean of the Lord, but of you? What if this time next year, I am writing to ask you for help in praise for an immense answer. WE SHALL SEE.

On February 14, 1878 Frances was able to write:

The twelve o'clock prayer [her customary practice] today was commuted into thanksgiving for completed work, so I write at once to tell you that the good Lord has given it me all, and fully answered the prayer that it might be done without difficulty or strain. I have now merely to put it straight for the press, fill in the references, and send it off. But the last sentence is written! I shall write no preface: the title is, *The Royal Invitation*, or, *Daily Thoughts on Coming to Christ*, and I prefer leaving it to the reader to find out who I am aiming at.

The Lord answered her prayer abundantly. He gave her the words He wanted her to write, and many copies were printed and sold. There is a Nisbet copy of *The Royal Invitation* with the printing number One Hundred and Eighty-third Thousand on the title page, and many more copies were published after that, by Nisbet and by American publishers. By the time *The Royal Invitation* was published, 30,000 copies of *My King* were already in circulation.

HOW WONDERFUL!

He answered all my prayer abundantly,
And crowned the work that to His feet I brought,
With blessing more than I had asked or thought—
A blessing undisguised, and fair, and free.

I stood amazed, and whispered, 'Can it be
  That He hath granted all the boon I sought?
  How wonderful that He for me hath wrought!
How wonderful that He hath answered me!'
O faithless heart! He said that He would hear
  And answer thy poor prayer, and He hath heard
And proved His promise. Wherefore didst thou fear?
  Why marvel that thy Lord hath kept His word?
More wonderful if He should fail to bless
Expectant faith and prayer with good success!

(*Under the Surface*)

– Inauguration of Mrs. Spurgeon's Book Fund –

The setting up of this Book Fund by Mrs. Spurgeon would not only benefit the Pastors, but also had a good result for *The Royal Books*, as we shall see. The way the fund came into being is reminiscent of an experience in Frances' life. As told in the final chapter of this book she realised 'in a flash' that she had the means to support the Church Missionary Society by way of sending most of her jewellery to Church House. Her desire to support the missionary cause was always uppermost in her thoughts, and she was glad of this opportunity given to her.

During the summer of 1875 C.H. Spurgeon completed the first volume of his *Lectures to my Students* and, having given a proof copy to his wife, asked her what she thought of the book. 'I wish I could place it in the hands of every minister in England' was the reply. The preacher at once rejoined, 'Then why not do so: how much will you give?' This was driving the nail home with a vengeance. Mrs. Spurgeon was not prepared for such a challenge, but she began to wonder if she could not spare the money from her housekeeping or personal account. It would necessitate pressure somewhere, she knew, for money was not plentiful just then.

Suddenly a flash of memory made the whole way clear:

Upstairs in a little drawer were some carefully hoarded crown pieces, which, owing to some foolish fancy, I had been gathering for years whenever chance threw one in my way; these I now counted out and found they made a sum exactly sufficient to pay for 100 copies of the work. If a twinge of regret at parting from my cherished but unwieldy favourites passed over me, it was gone in an instant, and then they were given freely and thankfully to the Lord, and in that moment though I knew it not, the Book Fund was inaugurated.

A follow-up from this is that in chapter ten of the biography *Life of Charles Haddon Spurgeon the World's Great Preacher* by Russell H. Cornwell (Philadelphia, Pennsylvania: Edgewood Publishing Co. 1892), the following appears:

> April, 1879—At the time of the Annual Conference of the Pastors' College the Book Fund usually prepares a little present for the three hundred pastors who then assemble. This is meant to be both a memorial of a happy gathering, and a pledge of continued interest in their welfare. This year, after due consideration, I have decided to give Miss Havergal's 'Royal' books (two to each pastor) as a choice and dainty morsel for their spiritual refreshment and quickening. No commendation is needed to insure a hearty welcome to a work by this devoted lady. Miss Havergal's pen is guided by a hand fast clasped in that of her Master, and therefore her simple words thrill to the inmost depths of the soul and touch many a hidden spring of tender, deep, religious feeling. I anticipate not only the pleasure with which our 'old students' will receive these delightful little books at my hands, but the abundant blessing they may bring to their hearts and homes. Through the kindness of Messrs. Nisbet, the publishers, I have been able to purchase a thousand copies, and having made it a matter of special prayer that not one of these precious seeds should be unfruitful, I shall hopefully and patiently await the result.

The above quote was written shortly before F.R.H.'s unexpected early death on June 3, 1879.

– *Continuing Impact* –

In her *Autobiography*, Frances' sister, Maria, tells of a visit she made to France in 1882, and while she was in Aix-les-Bains, she recounts:

> I met a woman resting her bundle, so I chatted awhile. She looked sad, and told me she had just said adieu to her husband and two dear little ones. He could not work, so she was going to Lyons to get in an hotel, and earn for them. I had no books with me, but said, 'If you will come to my hotel, I will give you one at 9 o'clock'. She hesitated, so I said, 'Will you come with me, then, now?' 'Oh yes'; so we had a long talk…

She sat down at the hotel while I wrote her name in F.'s *L'Invitation Royale*; it was delightful to send one to Lyons.

It was obvious that Frances' works were being distributed in various countries and in several languages. A friend was visiting Oakhampton House where Frances had lived and commented that:

> The circle of blessing from her life and lips is spreading wider and wider. Away over the stormy Atlantic her voice reaches with pleading tones, 'Will ye not come to Him for life? Why will ye die, oh why?' In the burning clime of India her sweet hymns are being given to the native converts in their own languages, and they fall as dew on the thirsting hearts. In sunny Switzerland the dark-eyed peasants still hear among their mountains the echoes of her clear voice singing— 'Que je sois, oh cher Sauveur, Seulement pour Toi!'.

Frances wrote the hymn in French while in Fins Haut in Switzerland. She had gathered a number of French peasant girls around her and, having spoken to them from the Bible, got them to sing this hymn. She had earlier seen these girls going to early mass and desired to tell them of the Lord Jesus Christ:

> I thought God could as well give me French as English, if He would, and I set to and wrote Seulement pour Toi…Only it is quite a different hymn, making prominent the other side; He and He only is and does all for us.

SEULEMENT POUR TOI

O that I be—May I be, O dear Saviour,
    Only [wholly] to Thee [Thine]!
Be the love of all my heart
    Solely for Thee.
I come back to my Father
    Only through Thee,
My confidence entire
    Wants to be [will be] in Thee,
    Only in Thee.

(first stanza; *'Under His Shadow'*)

WILL YOU NOT COME?

Will you not come to Him for *Life*?
 Why will ye die, oh why?
He gave His life for you, for you!
The gift is free, the word is true!
 Will you not come? Oh, why will you die?

Will you not come to Him for *Peace*?
 Peace through His cross alone!
He shed His precious blood for you;
The gift is free, the word is true!
 He is our Peace—oh, is He your own?

Will you not come to Him for *Rest*?
 All that are weary, come!
The rest He gives is deep and true;
'Tis offered now, 'tis offered you!
 Rest in His love, and rest in His home.

Will you not come to Him for *Joy*?
 Will you not come for this?
He laid His joys aside for you,
To give you joy, so sweet, so true!
 Sorrowing heart, oh, drink of the bliss!

Will you not come to Him for *Love*?
 Love that can fill the heart,
Exceeding great, exceeding free!
He loveth you, He loveth me!
 Will you not come? Why stand you apart?

Will you not come to Him for *ALL*?
 Will you not 'taste and see?'
He waits to give it all to you;
The gifts are free, the words are true!
 Jesus is calling, 'Come unto Me!'.

(Twenty-Fourth Day of *The Royal Invitation*)

Chapter Six

Behind Closed Doors

Thou art coming to a King,
Large petitions with thee bring;
For His grace and power are such,
None can ever ask too much.
John Newton

'Thy word have I hid in my heart...'
(Psalm 119:11)

*I*n the second volume of his *Works*, the Puritan Thomas Brooks speaks of 'closet prayer'. He is expounding Matthew 6:6, and having pointed out the benefits and indeed the necessity of spending time alone in prayer and meditation (in a room with the door shut), he suggests that Christians will make all manner of excuses not to engage in such activity.

> It is ten to one but that the objector every day fools away, or trifles away, or idles away, or sins away, one hour in a day, and why then should he object the want of time? There are none that toil...and busy themselves in their worldly employments, but do spend an hour or more in a day to little or no purpose, and busy themselves most in their worldly employments, either in gazing about...or in busying themselves in other men's matters, or in idle visits...And why then should not these men redeem an hour's time in a day for private prayer, out of that time which they usually spend so vainly and idly? Can you, notwithstanding all your great worldly employments, find an hour in the day...to play the fool in? And cannot you find an hour in the day to wait on God in your closets?

Those challenging words were written in the 17th century.

– *One Hour with Jesus* –

In the 19th century Frances Havergal wrote a piece entitled 'One Hour with Jesus' in which she expresses the same sentiments as those of Thomas Brooks two centuries earlier. The text she based her writing on was 'What! Could you not watch with Me one hour?' (Matt. 26:40) and she has this to say:

> Our Divine Master has called us to no Gethsemane watch of strange and mysterious darkness. It is while the brightness of the day is breaking—perhaps even long after it has broken—that His call to communion with Himself reaches our not always willing ear. 'Come with Me' (Song of Sol. 4:8), and the drowsy reply too often is, 'Presently Lord, not just this minute'.
>
> And then after 'yet a little sleep, a little slumber, a little folding of the hands to sleep' the precious hour is past which 'might have been' so full of blessing.
>
> A mere ten minutes—is that enough proportion for our warfare and provision for our wants; for spreading all our needs and difficulties before the Lord; for telling Jesus all that is in our hearts; for bringing before Him all the details of our work; for searching to know His mind and His will; for storing His word in our hearts; for replenishing our seed-baskets, that we may have something to sow, and getting Him to sharpen our sickles that we may reap; for confession and supplication and intercession, and, above all, for praise?
>
> Ten minutes or a quarter of an hour! Is that enough for the many things which He has to say to us? For the quiet teachings of His Spirit; for the dawning of His light on the dark sayings of old, and the flashing of His glory and power on the words which are spirit and life? Is that enough to spend in converse with the Friend of friends? Does this look as if we really cared very much about Him?

'All decays begin in the closet; no heart thrives without much secret converse with God; and nothing will make amends for the want of it'. (John Berridge)

'O! one hour with God infinitely exceeds all the pleasures and delights of this lower world'. (David Brainerd)

It is said that in the 20th century, Karl Barth used to spend the first hour of the day listening to the music of Mozart before he went into his study. Perhaps he had never read Brooks or Havergal!

– Bible Study –

Inevitably with prayer Frances linked the reading and meditation of the Scriptures. She loved her Bible and memorised all the New Testament (except the Book of Acts), all the Minor Prophets, Isaiah and all the Psalms, and probably many other individual chapters. This is why her works are so full of Scripture. Maria mentions in her *Memorials* that:

> It was at her study table that she read her Bible by seven o'clock in the summer and eight o'clock in winter; her Hebrew Bible, Greek Testament, and lexicons being at hand. Sometimes on bitterly cold mornings, I begged that she would read with her feet comfortably to the fire, and received the reply: 'But then, Marie, I can't rule my lines neatly; just see what a find I've got! If one only searches, there are such extraordinary things in the Bible!'

An interesting study Frances made of the Unity in Diversity of the Scriptures is given in *Starlight Through the Shadows*. She notes the book of Proverbs seems to be an epitome of the lessons to be learnt from the whole of Scripture history; or the history as a volume of illustrations of the Proverbs. For example, compare:

2 Chronicles 1:10	Proverbs 4:5-7
Give me now wisdom and knowledge, that I may go out and come in before this people: for who can judge this thy people, that is so great?	Get wisdom, get understanding: forget it not; neither decline from the words of my mouth. Forsake her not, and she shall preserve thee: love her, and she shall keep thee. Wisdom is the principal thing; therefore get wisdom: and with all thy getting get understanding.

2 Chronicles 1:12	Proverbs 3:16
Wisdom and knowledge is granted unto thee; and I will give thee riches, and wealth, and honour, such as none of the kings have had that have been before thee, neither shall there any after thee have the like.	Length of days is in her right hand; and in her left hand riches and honour.

2 Chronicles 2:3	Proverbs 27:10
And Solomon sent to Huram the king of Tyre, saying, "As thou didst deal with David my father, and didst send him cedars to build him an house to dwell therein, even so deal with me."	Thine own friend, and thy father's friend, forsake not; neither go into thy brother's house in the day of thy calamity: for better is a neighbour that is near than a brother far off.

Frances thought that the morality of the Proverbs is identical with that of the New Testament. The precepts of the former generally occur as statements in the latter, and vice versa; e.g. compare:

Proverbs 3:9	1 Corinthians 16:2
Honour the LORD with thy substance, and with the firstfruits of all thine increase:	Upon the first day of the week let every one of you lay by him in store, as God hath prospered him, that there be no gatherings when I come.

Proverbs 3:28	Matthew 5:42
Say not unto thy neighbour, "Go, and come again, and tomorrow I will give;" when thou hast it by thee.	Give to him that asketh thee, and from him that would borrow of thee turn not thou away.

Proverbs 8:13	Romans 12:9
The fear of the LORD is to hate evil: pride, and arrogancy, and the evil way, and the froward mouth, do I hate.	Let love be without dissimulation. Abhor that which is evil; cleave to that which is good.

She also maintained that every book in the New Testament has some parallel in Proverbs, some chapters (e.g. Romans 12, James 4) having parallels with nearly every verse.

A mind well furnished with Scripture, which has spent time in meditation on its teaching, and is convinced of the power of the Author, will see through all hypocritical objections to Christian faith, and be able to contend for the faith which has been given to the church (Sinclair Ferguson in *Let's Study Mark*, Edinburgh: Banner of Truth Trust, 2005, p. 198).

- Standing Firm -

There were times in Frances Havergal's life when she certainly stood her ground as far as the truth was concerned. Her sister Maria wrote this account:

> Once when she was about to converse with a clergyman, she said, 'Marie, when an hour is up, come in'. There was F., her hand waving, and I just caught this characteristic end of her talk, 'Oh, why don't you preach the gospel of Christ?' Answer, 'My congregation are well-educated and well acquainted with the truths of salvation; if they were Zulus, I should preach differently'. F., 'Then I will be a Zulu next Sunday, and just preach at me!' To her delight, a real gospel sermon was the result.

In the top left corner of the blank left-side page facing the title page of her Bagster Study Bible she wrote:

> If we believe in the Revealer,
> We have no difficulty about the Revelation.

At the top of the title page of the New Testament, F.R.H. copied this quotation of Augustine:

> The New Testament is enfolded in the Old, and the Old Testament is unfolded in the New.

At the top of Hebrews 11 in the margin she wrote:

> With the world, seeing is believing:
> With the Christian, believing is seeing.

Frances used the system of marking her Bible as recommended by a friend, Mrs. Stephen Menzies. This involved underlining and 'railways' as can be seen from the illustration of a page from Frances' Bible on Psalm 119 (See photograph 12). Apparently only one objection was raised against this method: viz., the peculiar appearance which the pages presented when crossed by the 'railways'. But that was regarded as a small price to pay for the advantages gained.

One of Frances' writings was her 'Bible Study for the Sundays of the Year'. Here are two random selections:

THIRTY-EIGHTH WEEK

For June 2. Hosea 13:9. 'In ME is thine help', not merely 'I will help thee' Psalm 89:19. Then I was thinking of looking out all the other things which we have 'in Him', e.g. Isaiah 45:24; Ephesians 1:7, 11; John 16:33 etc. but not time to work them out this morning.

FIFTY-SECOND WEEK

In Exodus 15, verse 13 was given me if ever one was, and has been delicious food all the week, every word so peculiarly full of power and beauty to me. 'Thou IN THY MERCY hast led forth the people which Thou HAST REDEEMED. Thou hast guided them IN THY STRENGTH UNTO Thy holy habitation'. I have only time to glance at Exodus 22, for Sunday, but what catches my eye is verse 20, 'Unto the Lord ONLY'. It brings up the whole subject of 'only for Jesus'—the sacrifices of praise, love, bodies (Romans 12:1), 'selves', etc. all 'unto the Lord only'.

– *Regular Bible Reading Recommended* –

A Postscript was added by F.R.H. to *Royal Bounty* in which she encouraged her readers to a regular reading of the Bible—going straight through.

…Regularly, not only as to constancy, but as to system. How much time is wasted in indecision, and wondering what to read next! How many are familiar only with their favourite parts of God's Word, neglecting others almost entirely; thus overlooking many a Royal Commandment, and losing much of His Royal Bounty…we ought to be reading both parts of His Word regularly every day.

– *Fruits of Study* –

When Frances was in Switzerland in 1876 she was reading through Exodus and came to the passage in chapter 21, verses 5 and 6. This concerns a law whereby a slave was given the right to go free in the seventh year or remain with his master if he so wished. The thought so gripped her that she frequently returned to the theme of 'My Master' in her works, and the words of the following hymn came flowing into her mind:

MY MASTER

I love, I love my Master,
    I will not go out free,
For He is my Redeemer;
    He paid the price for me.

I would not leave His service,
    It is so sweet and blest;
And in the weariest moments
    He gives the truest rest.

My Master shed His life-blood
    My vassal life to win,
And save me from the bondage
    Of tyrant self and sin.

He chose me for His service,
    And gave me power to choose
That blessed, perfect freedom,
    Which I shall never lose.

I would not halve my service,
    His *only* it must be!
His only, Who so loved me,
    And gave Himself for me.

Rejoicing and adoring,
    Henceforth my song shall be,
I love, I love my Master,
    I will not go out free.

(partial quotation; Twenty-Fourth Day of *Loyal Responses*)

Frances' life shows that she loved to study God's Word and found it richly rewarding. Her delight was in the law of the Lord and it was always her standard of appeal. She was also eager that others should find that same delight, and encouraged them to search the Scriptures.

The following song was written a few weeks before she died:

THE SCRIPTURE CANNOT BE BROKEN

Upon the Word I rest,
   Each pilgrim day;
This golden staff is best
   For all the way.
What Jesus Christ hath spoken,
   Can*not* be broken!

Upon the Word I rest,
   So strong, so sure,
So full of comfort blest,
   So sweet, so pure!
The charter of salvation,
   Faith's broad foundation.

Upon the Word I stand!
   That cannot die!
Christ seals it in my hand
   He cannot lie!
The word that faileth never!
   Abiding ever!

Chorus:
The Master hath said it! Rejoicing in this,
   We ask not for sign or for token;
His word is enough for our confident bliss—
   'The Scripture *cannot* be broken!'

(*Closing Chords*)

Chapter Seven

Onward and Upward

JANUARY 5TH

Now onward, ever onward, 'from strength to strength' we go,
While 'grace for grace' abundantly shall from His fulness flow,
To glory's full fruition, from glory's foretaste here,
Until His very Presence crown our happiest New Year!

(*Red Letter Days*)

'Onward, upward, homeward!' I shall soon be there,
Soon its joys and pleasures, I, through grace, shall share.
'Onward, upward, homeward!' Come along with me:
Ye who love the Saviour, bear me company;
'Onward, upward, homeward!' press with vigour on,
Yet a little moment, and the race is won!

Albert Midlane

$\mathcal{R}$eading through the life of Frances Havergal reveals that she had known much spiritual blessing and usefulness. She was gratefully conscious of having for many years loved the Lord and delighted in His service, but she felt there was something more to the Christian life than she had known.

In December 1873 Frances had a spiritual experience that was of deep significance to her and had a transforming effect upon her life. It occurred after she had read a little book sent to her entitled *All for Jesus* written by the Rev. J. T. Wrenford, a minister in Newport, Monmouthshire. The contents went straight to her need and longing, and she replied to the writer, 'I do so long for deeper and fuller teaching in my own heart. "All for Jesus" has touched me very much…I know I love Jesus, and there are times when I feel such intensity of love to Him that I have not words to describe it. I rejoice, too, in Him as my Master and Sovereign, but I want to come nearer still…to know the power of His resurrection, even if it be with the fellowship of His sufferings. And all this, not exactly for my own joy alone, but for others'.

In reply, Wrenford mentioned 1 John 1:7 and pointed out the power of Jesus to keep those who abide in Him from falling, and that the blood of Jesus Christ goes on cleansing from all sin. She replied, 'I see it all, and I HAVE the blessing'.

> Yes, it was on Advent Sunday, December 2, 1873, I first saw clearly the blessedness of true consecration. I saw it as a flash of electric light, and what you see you can never unsee…There must be full surrender before there can be full blessedness…And then as to sanctification: that it is the work of the Holy Spirit and progressive, is the very thing I see and rejoice in. He has brought me into the 'highway of holiness', up which I trust every day to progress, continually pressing forward, led by the Spirit of God.
>
> But, understand me, it is not as though I had already attained, either were already perfect; but I follow after, I press toward the mark for the prize of the high calling of God in Christ Jesus.

At the Keswick Convention in 1951, Mr. Fred Mitchell was speaking on 'The Mystical Union of Christ and the Believer', expounding John 14:20——'At that day ye shall know that I am in My Father, and ye in Me, and I in you'. He mentions that the union with Christ is real and deep and we may say with Paul that 'I live; yet not I, but Christ liveth in me'. He goes on to quote Frances Ridley Havergal:

HE IS THY LIFE

Jesus, my life is Thine,
And evermore shall be
Hidden in Thee!
For nothing can untwine,
Thy life from mine.

(sixth stanza; Twentieth Day of *Loyal Responses*)

During the early 1870s, certain teaching on holiness and the 'higher life' came into prominence, with the Keswick Convention being formed in 1875. The 'holiness movement' had swept across America and penetrated into England where its influence was evident in the Moody and Sankey meetings around that time. Frances certainly agreed with the fact of consecration as distinct from conversion, but was not happy to go along with the 'higher life' emphasis. This was the reason why she would not go to the Keswick Convention lest it gave the wrong impression.

She clearly stated her views on the teaching of sinless perfection:

> As to 'perfectionism' or 'sinlessness', I have all along, and over and over again, said I never did, and do not hold either. 'Sinlessness' belongs only to Christ now, and to our glorified state in heaven. I believe it to be not merely an impossibility on earth, but an actual contradiction of our very being, which cannot be sinless till the resurrection change has passed upon us. But being kept from falling, kept from sins, is quite another thing, and the Bible seems to teem with commands and promises about it.

- A Surrendered Will -

In late January 1874 Frances was apparently expecting a letter from her American publisher containing a cheque now due to her, and also good news about some other work waiting to be published. The letter arrived but brought the news that 'my publisher has failed in the universal crash'. It seems he held the copyright of some of her works and she foresaw the end of her American contacts. Her comment was:

> Two months ago this would have been a real trial to me, for I had built a good deal on my American prospects; now 'Thy will be done' is not a sigh but a song...The sense of His unutterable loving kindness to me is simply overwhelming.

Then in 1876 something else occurred in Frances' life that could have caused her even greater distress. She had been helping her friend and co-worker, the Rev. Charles B. Snepp, prepare a manuscript for the Appendix to *Songs of Grace and Glory*—a hymn book which they had been compiling together. After much diligence to complete the many sheets of manuscript music she was able to send them to the printers: 'There, it is all done and now I am free to write a book'.

A week later she was informed by the printer that there had been a fire at his premises and the whole of her work had been destroyed. For other work she had done she had kept a copy, but as it had never been required, she did not feel it necessary to do so in this instance, especially as it had to be laboriously copied by hand. Having learnt of the disaster, however, she testified that she was again able to say, 'Thy way, not mine, O Lord', and proceeded to work through the next six months to reproduce it. She was sure there was a purpose in it all.

HITHERTO AND HENCEFORTH
'The Lord hath blessed me hitherto'—Joshua 17:14

> HITHERTO the Lord hath helped us,
>   Guiding all the way;
> Henceforth let us trust Him fully,
>   Trust Him all the day.
>
> Hitherto the Lord hath loved us,
>   Caring for His own;
> Henceforth let us love Him better,
>   Live for Him alone.
>
> Hitherto the Lord hath blessed us,
>   Crowning all our days;
> Henceforth let us live to bless Him,
>   Live to show His praise.

(*Home Words*)

- *Frances and the Mildmay Mission* -

In 1864 a godly vicar, William Pennefather, moved from Barnet to St. Jude's, Mildmay Park. No one spoke of him as a talented man, but as a holy man, wholly consecrated to his Master. Frances had a great regard for him and referred to his hymns as reflecting his inner life which resulted in his outer life of daily dependence on

God. (She was also very pleased that Pennefather was a 'pledged supporter' of her beloved Irish Society!)

Under his auspices the Mildmay Institution was founded on the basis that he believed in preaching the Word in its fulness and meeting the practical needs of the people. The Institution was known for a variety of enterprises, including hospitals, orphanages and schools—directed mostly towards the poorest sections of society. In 1866 a ten-bed cottage hospital was set up in Mildmay Park which was followed in 1874 with the opening of a medical mission in Turville Street.

A yearly Conference was introduced later which was attended by people from all parts of the kingdom and overseas. Many testified to the threefold blessing which always seemed granted: personal joy in the Lord, increase of desire for personal holiness and increase of zeal and power for work.

Although Frances was only able to attend one Conference, she was a member of the Association of Female Workers connected with the Institution, and in 1874 was able to go to one of their quarterly meetings. 'It is a sort of dream to be at Mildmay; it is very delicious.' Having met there Mrs. Hudson Taylor from China, she wrote with great fervour, 'It is such a privilege to be one of such an Association. And you don't see a dismal face among them! And they are so affectionate, the Sun is so bright that there's no ice left to be broken.'

While attending another of these quarterly meetings she caught a feverish cold and knowing that she would have to stay for a while, hoped to go into the Mildmay Home for Invalids which she quite fancied.

> But they would not let me get into a cold cab...so I resigned myself to an extra week here. And, verily, they do know how to nurse, and, what's more (!), how to keep you quiet. Also they do know how to pray! I have learnt a little, I hope, on that subject this last week.

Frances was visited daily by Mrs. Pennefather and she wrote to her step-mother at the time: 'I see that the more one knows her, the more one must love her'.

Frances did not become directly involved with the Mildmay Mission's work among the poor of London, but she did take an active interest in the Flower Mission which organised the distribution of posies and cards with Bible texts to the sick in city hospitals. On one occasion Frances sent off about 380 little bouquets to this Mission, over half of which were gathered and made up by the servants at Oakhampton. 'Some of the nosegays were lovely, and the ensemble when got together ready to pack, was quite a sight'. Cards, inscribed with a single Bible verse or series of verses surrounded by colourful floral decorations, were particularly popular in the Victorian era, and there can have been few middle-class homes in the country that did not receive each year at least one F.R.H. card, as well as the hospitals. Even during her lifetime these little cards were being issued in tens of thousands, and their popularity continued and increased after her death.

To finish the story of the Mildmay Institution, in 1890 the foundations were laid of a new purpose-built hospital, and in 1892 it was erected as a memorial to William Pennefather. It was to be known as the Mildmay Mission Hospital. For many years it was the place that missionaries would visit on furlough when they required medical help or recuperation from their labours. The history of the ensuing years, from threatened closure, to actual closure, to re-opening is told in *The Birth and Rebirth of a Unique Hospital*, available from Mildmay Mission Hospital, Hackney Road, London E2 7NA, UK, and reaches to the present day with its aim of improving HIV/ AIDS care in the United Kingdom and, in particular, Africa. So it has come full circle from being founded as a strong evangelical Institution in Frances' day, to going through the doldrums during the 1930s and 40s, and then emerging to be a renowned evangelical medical centre and worldwide witness to the compassion of Christ in the 21st century.

Frances received much blessing from her connection with Mildmay and would no doubt have been encouraged to know that it still has a ministry today, not only in the Hospital in London but also in other parts of the world.

FOR NEW YEAR'S DAY, 1874

'From glory unto glory!' What mighty blessings crown
The lives for which our Lord hath laid His own so freely down!
Omnipotence to keep us, Omniscience to guide,
Jehovah's Triune Presence within us to abide!

The fulness of His blessing encompasseth our way;
The fulness of His promises crowns every brightening day;
The fulness of His glory is beaming from above,
While more and more we realize the fulness of His love.

'In full and glad surrender we give ourselves to Thee,
Thine utterly, and only, and evermore to be!
O Son of God, who lov'st us, we will be Thine alone,
And all we are, and all we have, shall henceforth be thine own!'

Now, onward, ever onward, from 'strength to strength' we go,
While 'grace for grace' abundantly shall from His fulness flow,
To glory's full fruition, from glory's foretaste here,
Until His Very Presence crown our happiest New Year!

(partial quotation; *Under the Surface*)

RESTING

Resting on the faithfulness of Christ our Lord,
Resting on the fulness of His own sure word,
Resting on His power, on His love untold;
Resting on His covenant secured of old.

Resting and believing, let us onward press;
Resting in Himself, the Lord our Righteousness;
Resting and rejoicing, let His saved ones sing,
Glory, glory, glory be to Christ our King!

(first and fifth stanzas; Sixteenth Day of *Loyal Responses*)

Chapter Eight

A Hymn Selection

It is likely that the name of Frances Ridley Havergal is best known today through her hymns, even though they are only a small part of her writings. A selection is given here with some details of their origin.

One of her earliest hymns was written in Germany in 1859 during a return visit to the Pastor with whom she had stayed previously. Coming in weary one day, she sat down and noticed on the wall a picture of Christ on the cross. This moved her greatly, especially when she read the motto underneath: 'I gave My life for thee; what hast thou given for Me?' Some lines flashed through her mind, and she wrote them down in pencil. But not being satisfied with them, she threw the paper into the fire, but it fell out merely singed.

When Frances showed the hymn to her father some months later, he gave warm approval and wrote the tune *Baca* for it. The following three verses give the challenge she felt:

I DID THIS FOR THEE! WHAT HAST THOU DONE FOR ME?

> I gave My life for thee,
>   My precious blood I shed
> That thou might'st ransomed be,
>   And quickened from the dead.
> I gave My life for thee
> What hast thou given for Me?
>
> And I have brought to thee
>   Down from My home above,
> Salvation full and free,

My pardon and my love.
Great gifts I brought to thee:
What hast thou brought to Me?

Oh, let thy life be given,
    Thy years for Him be spent;
World-fetters all be riven,
    And joy with suffering blent.
I gave Myself for thee:
Give thou thyself to Me!

(*The Ministry of Song*)

Years later Frances wrote 'To Thee', as a response to the Saviour's love.

TO THEE

I bring my sins to Thee,
    The sins I cannot count,
That all may cleansed be
    In Thy once opened fount.
I bring them, Saviour, all to Thee:
The burden is too great for me.

My heart to Thee I bring,
    The heart I cannot read,
A faithless, wandering thing,
    An evil heart indeed.
I bring it, Saviour, now to Thee,
That fixed and faithful it may be.

My joys to Thee I bring—
    The joys Thy love hath given,
That each may be a wing
    To lift me nearer heaven.
I bring them, Saviour, all to Thee,
For Thou hast purchased all for me.

My life I bring to Thee,
    I would not be my own;
O Saviour let me be
    Thine ever, Thine alone!
My heart, my life, my all I bring
To Thee, my Saviour, and my King.

(partial quotation; *Under the Surface*)

* * * * * *

Frances lived near the river Severn for most of her days. At Astley, Dick Brook flowed into it, and while in Worcester she enjoyed walking along the river banks. When in Winterdyne (her sister Ellen's home) she could see it flowing below the woods 'with an extra sparkle and glitter and shine'.

PERFECT PEACE

Like a river glorious
    Is God's perfect peace,
Over all victorious
    In its bright increase;
Perfect—yet it floweth
    Fuller every day;
Perfect—yet it groweth
    Deeper all the way.

Hidden in the hollow
    Of His blessed hand,
Never foe can follow,
    Never traitor stand.
Not a surge of worry,
    Not a shade of care,
Not a blast of hurry
    Touch the spirit there.

Every joy or trial
    Falleth from above,
Traced upon our dial
    By the Sun of love.
We may trust Him fully
    All for us to do;
They who trust Him wholly
    Find Him wholly true.

Chorus:
Stayed upon Jehovah,
    Hearts are fully blest,
Finding, as He promised,
    Perfect peace and rest.

(Twenty-Fifth Day of *Loyal Responses*)

This hymn was written in 1874 while she was staying with Maria in Leamington. One can almost imagine her lying in bed and, recalling the peaceful serenity of this river, expressing her thoughts very vividly—thankful that she knew the Lord's peace in the midst of her pain.

* * * * * *

Probably the most familiar of all Frances' hymns is the one known as the 'Consecration Hymn', written in 1874. We have an account from her as to how it came to be written:

Perhaps you will be interested to know the origin of the consecration hymn, 'Take my life'. I went for a little visit of five days [to friends in Stourport]. There were ten persons in the house, some unconverted and long prayed for, some converted but not rejoicing Christians. He gave me the prayer, 'Lord give me all in this house!'. And He just did! Before I left the house every one had got a blessing. The last night of my visit I was too happy to sleep, and passed most of the night in praise and renewal of my own consecration, and these little couplets formed themselves and chimed in my heart one after another, till they finished with, Ever, only, all for Thee!'

CONSECRATION HYMN

Take my life and let it be
Consecrated, Lord, to Thee;

Take my moments and my days,
Let them flow in ceaseless praise.

Take my hands and let them move
At the impulse of Thy love;

Take my feet, and let them be
Swift and beautiful for Thee.

Take my voice and let me sing
Always, only, for my King;

Take my lips, and let them be
Filled with messages from Thee.

Take my silver and my gold,
Not a mite would I withhold;

Take my intellect, and use
Every power as Thou shalt choose.

Take my will and make it Thine;
It shall be no longer mine;

Take my heart, it is Thine own;
It shall be Thy royal throne.

Take my love, my Lord, I pour
At Thy feet its treasure store;

Take myself, and I will be
Ever, only, ALL, for Thee.

(First Day of *Loyal Responses*)

Frances commented, 'I particularly wish that hymn kept to my father's sweet little tune, *Patmos*, which suits it perfectly'.

Perhaps it is worth noting that such an eminent and helpful commentator as William Hendriksen did not hesitate to quote some stanzas from this hymn in his *Commentary on Luke* on the subject of consecration.

There had obviously been some criticism of her hymn, and she wrote to a friend:

...I suppose it was the 'silver and gold' line that was objected to; and I do think that couplet 'Take my silver and my gold, Not a mite would I withhold' is peculiarly liable to be objected to by those who do not really understand the spirit of it, don't you? So I am not a bit surprised! Yes, 'not a mite would I withhold'; but that does not mean that, because we have ten shillings in our purse, we are pledged to put it all into the next collecting plate, else we should have none for the next call! But it does mean that every shilling is to be, and I think I may say is, held at my Lord's disposal, and is distinctly not my own; but, as He has entrusted to me a body for my special charge, I am bound to clothe that body with His silver and gold, so that it shall neither suffer from cold, nor bring discredit upon His cause!

With the same common sense, she explains her reasons for dressing as she did:

The outer should be the expression of the inner, not an ugly mask or disguise. If the King's daughter is to be 'all glorious within', she must not be outwardly a fright! I must dress both as a lady and a Christian. The question of cost I see very strongly, and do not consider myself at liberty to spend on dress that which might be spared for God's work: but it costs no more to have a thing well and prettily made...When working among strangers, if I dressed below par, it would attract attention and might excite opposition; by dressing unremarkably, and yet with a generally pleasing effect, no attention is distracted. Also, what is suitable in one house is not so in another, and it would be almost an insult to appear at dinner among some of my relatives and friends in what I could wear without apology at home; it would be an actual breach of the rule 'Be courteous'; also, I should not think it right to appear among wedding guests in a dress which would be perfectly suitable for wearing to the Infirmary. But I shall always ask for guidance in all things!

* * * * * *

Once when reading 1 Peter 1:8, 'Whom having not seen, ye love', Frances was able to express her thoughts in the following hymn—she loved to sing the praises of her Saviour:

OUR KING

O Saviour, precious Saviour,
　　Whom yet unseen we love;
O Name of might and favour,
　　All other names above!

We worship Thee, we bless Thee,
To Thee alone we sing;
We praise Thee, and confess Thee
Our holy Lord and King!

In Thee all fulness dwelleth,
All grace and power divine;
The glory that excelleth,
O Son of God, is Thine:
We worship Thee, we bless Thee,
To Thee alone we sing;
We praise Thee, and confess Thee
Our glorious Lord and King!

(first and third stanzas, *Under the Surface*)

* * * * * *

Frances wrote a 'Second Advent Song' while at Winterdyne in November 1873. It had been written in response to a request from her friend, the Rev. Charles B. Snepp, for a hymn on the theme 'Good Master'. Finding herself unable to meet his exact requirements, she wrote explaining this, and added:

He has just given me something else instead—'*Thou art coming, O my Saviour*'. It is a hymn of praise to Christ, glorying in his many roles— Saviour, King, Priest, Lord, Master, and Friend—but from the last verse it is evident that the dominant theme is the enthronement and sovereignty of Christ the King:

ADVENT SONG

Thou art coming, O my Saviour!
Thou art coming, O my King!
In Thy beauty all-resplendent,
In Thy glory all-transcendent;
Well may we rejoice and sing!
Coming! in the opening east,
Herald brightness slowly swells;
Coming! O my glorious Priest,
Hear we not Thy golden bells?

Not a cloud and not a shadow,
Not a mist and not a tear,
Not a sin and not a sorrow,
Not a dim and veiled tomorrow,
For that sunrise grand and clear!
Jesus Saviour, once with Thee,
Nothing else seems worth a thought!
Oh, how marvellous will be
All the bliss Thy pain hath bought!

Oh, the joy to see Thee reigning,
Thee, my own beloved Lord!
Every tongue Thy name confessing,
Worship, honour, glory, blessing,
Brought to Thee with glad accord!
Thee, my Master and my Friend,
Vindicated and enthroned!
Unto earth's remotest end
Glorified, adored, and owned!

(partial quotation; *Under the Surface*)

Neither she nor her father held the pre-millennial doctrine then popular among many of their evangelical friends, but she believed confidently that Scripture pointed to one final coming again of Christ in glory on the Last Day of the world. Maria recalled in her *Autobiography*: 'I remember my sister F. with her exceeding common sense ending a long discussion by many strong pre-millennialists— all differing widely—"I think, when our dear Lord does come, not one of you will be able to say, 'there, I told you it would be so!'"'.

* * * * * *

The 'Ascension Song' quoted at the end of this book was written in December 1871 while she was staying at Perry Barr with her friends, the Rev. and Mrs. Charles B. Snepp. She was accompanying Mr. Snepp on his pastoral visiting, and walked to the boys' schoolroom with him. Being rather tired, however, she leaned against the playground wall while her friend went in to speak to the children. On his return a little while later he found her scribbling on an old envelope. At his request she gave him the hymn which she had just pencilled in—'Golden harps are sounding'. She later composed the tune *Hermas* for it:

* * * * * *

Frances' missionary zeal, commemorated by the formation of the Frances Ridley Havergal 'Church Missionary Memorial Fund' a few weeks after her death, is shown in her lively hymn 'Tell it Out!' It was written at Winterdyne one snowy Sunday morning when she was unable to go to church. As she afterwards said, "In reading the Psalms for the day I came to 'Tell it out among the heathen that the Lord is King', and I thought, what a splendid first line! And then words and music came rushing in to me."

When the churchgoers returned, hymn and harmonies were all beautifully written out. The following is the first verse:

TELL IT OUT!

Tell it out among the heathen that the Lord is King!
Tell it out! Tell it out!
Tell it out among the nations, bid them shout and sing!
Tell it out! Tell it out!
Tell it out with adoration, that He shall increase;
That the mighty King of glory is the King of peace;
Tell it out with jubilation though the waves may roar,
That He sitteth on the water-floods, our King for evermore!
Tell it out, etc.

(*Under the Surface*)

This hymn is not in many of today's hymnbooks, but it was very popular among Frances' missionary-minded friends. She would sing it herself when wanting to encourage people to speak of the Saviour.

*   *   *   *   *   *

'I am trusting Thee, Lord Jesus' was written at Ormont Dessous, Switzerland in September 1874. It was known to be her own favourite, and was found in her pocket Bible after her death:

TRUSTING

I am trusting Thee, Lord Jesus,
Trusting only Thee;
Trusting Thee for full salvation,
Great and free.

I am trusting Thee for pardon,
At Thy feet I bow,
For Thy grace and tender mercy,
Trusting now.

I am trusting Thee for cleansing,
In the crimson flood;
Trusting Thee to make me holy
By Thy blood.

I am trusting Thee to guide me;
  Thou alone must lead!
Every day and hour supplying
  All my need.

I am trusting Thee for power,
  Thine can never fail!
Words which Thou thyself shalt give me,
  Must prevail.

I am trusting Thee, Lord Jesus:
  Never let me fall!
I am trusting Thee for ever,
  And for all.

(Twelfth Day of *Loyal Responses*)

* * * * * *

Frances' *Letters* give some interesting insights into her contacts across the world. Once in 1875, when she was recuperating in Whitby after a very serious illness, she wrote to an American friend who had invited her to the American Women's Christian Association at New York. Her friend had also requested, if she was not able to come, that she write a poem to be read at the Conference and also printed. At first Frances was going to decline both offers, but then the following hymn came to her when someone suggested that those 'who have cast all our care on Him are under a sort of delusion.' Frances said, 'It made me so very glad to feel that it was no delusion, but that He does take every bit of my care, that it seemed as if my tongue, or rather pen, was loosed again, and I could not help a little gush of praise and testimony for the first time since my long illness'.

WITHOUT CAREFULNESS

Master! how shall I bless Thy name
  For Thy tender love to me,
For the sweet enablings of Thy grace,
  So sovereign, yet so free,
That have taught me to obey Thy word
  And cast my care on Thee!

'No anxious thought upon thy brow
    The watching world should see;
No carefulness! O child of God,
    For *nothing* careful be!
But cast thou *all* thy care on Him
    Who always cares for thee.'

How shall I praise Thee, Saviour dear,
    For this new life so sweet,
For taking all the care I laid
    At Thy belovèd feet,
Keeping Thy hand upon my heart
    To still each anxious beat!

I long to praise Thee more, and yet
    This is no care to me:
If Thou shalt fill my mouth with songs,
    Then I shall sing to Thee;
And if my silence praise Thee best,
    Then silent I will be.

Yet if it be Thy will, dear Lord,
    Oh, send me forth, to be
Thy messenger to careful hearts,
    To bid them taste, and see
How good Thou art to those who cast
    All, all their care on Thee!

(partial quotation; Twenty-Eighth Day of *Loyal Responses*)

*   *   *   *   *   *

Following Scripture, one of Frances' ways of describing the role of the Christian was that of the soldier. This hymn was written in October 1877, and we quote one verse:

ON THE LORD'S SIDE

Who is on the Lord's side?
    Who will serve the King?
Who will be His helpers
    Other lives to bring?

Who will leave the world's side?
Who will face the foe?
Who is on the Lord's side?
Who for Him will go?

Chorus:
By Thy call of mercy,
By Thy grace divine,
We are on the Lord's side;
Saviour, we are Thine.

(first verse; Fifth Day of *Loyal Responses*)

Writing to a young friend she challenged him with the words: 'It is a grand thing to start out early and be on the Lord's side all along. Oh, what an amount of sorrow it will save you if He gives you grace to do it...don't wait'.

* * * * * *

Another known favourite that she wrote is the very meditative communion hymn where faith, hope and love are joined around the Cross. The Communion service was of great significance to Frances, and she always observed it with much seriousness:

UNDER HIS SHADOW

Sit down beneath His shadow,
And rest with great delight;
The faith that now beholds Him
Is pledge of future sight.

Our Master's love remember,
Exceeding great and free;
Lift up thy heart in gladness,
For He remembers thee.

A little while, though parted,
Remember, wait, and love;
Until He comes in glory,
Until we meet above;

Till in the Father's kingdom
The heavenly feast is spread,
And we behold His beauty
Whose blood for us was shed!

(partial quotation; *Under the Surface*)

*   *   *   *   *   *

Starlight Through the Shadows was written for invalids a few months before Frances died, and the text she based her meditation on in chapter five was 'Him with whom we have to do' (Hebrews 4:13):

> These words seem to meet every sort of need of comfort. If it is perplexity, or oppressive puzzle what to do, when we cannot see through things—or if it is being unable to explain yourself to others, and trials or complications arising out of this: just fall back upon 'Him with whom we have to do'.

Having sought to show that Jesus is Guide, Shield and High Priest and is to be depended on above all others, Frances closes the chapter with several verses of the following hymn:

I COULD NOT DO WITHOUT THEE

I could not do without Thee,
O Saviour of the lost;
Whose precious blood redeemed me
At such tremendous cost;
Thy righteousness, Thy pardon,
Thy precious blood must be
My only hope and comfort,
My glory and my plea.

I could not do without Thee,
I cannot stand alone;
I have no strength nor goodness,
No wisdom of my own.
But Thou, beloved Saviour,
Art all in all to me,
And perfect strength in weakness
Is theirs who lean on Thee.

I could not do without Thee,
  O Jesus, Saviour dear!
E'en when my eyes are holden,
  I know that Thou art near.
How dreary and how lonely
  This changeful life would be,
Without the sweet communion,
  The secret rest with Thee!

I could not do without Thee,
  No other friend can read
The spirit's strange deep longings,
  Interpreting its need.
No human heart could enter
  Each dim recess of mine
And soothe and hush and calm it,
  O blessed Lord, but Thine.

I could not do without Thee,
  For years are fleeting fast,
And soon in solemn loneness
  The river must be passed.
But Thou wilt never leave me,
  And though the waves roll high,
I know Thou wilt be near me
  And whisper, It is I.

(partial quotation; *Under the Surface*)

Chapter Nine

The Younger Generation

Wherewithal shall a young man
cleanse his way?
By taking heed thereto according to thy word.
(Psalm 119:9)

Frances had a deep love for children and a strong desire for them to know and love 'her Master'. Her nephews and nieces were especially dear to her, and she sent many letters to them encouraging them to read the Bible and pray. The works she wrote with the young in mind were very perceptive and never condescending: they reveal her longing to be of use to them in a practical way in guiding their thoughts and lives in the right paths.

Attention has already been drawn in another chapter to Frances' little book *Bruey*, and it would be so good if that could be republished. But there are others such as *Little Pillows*, and she writes an introduction as to how the book came to be written:

A little girl was away from home on a week's visit. We will suppose her name was Ethel. The first night, when she was tucked up in bed, and just ready for a good night kiss, I said, 'Now, shall I give you a little pillow?'. Ethel lifted her head to see what was under it, and said, 'I have got one, Auntie!'

'It was another sort of pillow that I meant to give you; I wonder if you will like it?' So then Ethel saw it was not a question of feathers and pillow-case; still she did not understand, and so she laughed and said, 'Do tell me at once, Auntie, what you mean; don't keep me waiting to guess!'

Then I told her that, just as we wanted a nice soft pillow to lay our heads down upon at night, our hearts wanted a pillow too, something to rest upon, some true, sweet word that we might go to sleep upon happily and peacefully. And that it was a good plan always to take a little text for our pillow every night. So she had one that night, and the next night.

The third night I was prevented from coming up till long after Ethel ought to have been asleep. But there were the bright eyes peeping out robin-redbreast fashion, and a reproachful little voice said, 'Auntie, you have not given me any little pillow tonight!'

'Then, do you really care about having the little pillows given you, Ethel?'

'Oh, of course I do!' was the answer. She did not seem to think there could possibly be any doubt about it. Certainly the way in which she said that 'of course' showed that she had no doubt about it!

So it seemed that perhaps other little ones would like to have 'little pillows' put ready for every night. For even little hearts are sometimes very weary, and want something to rest upon; and a happy little heart, happy in the love of Jesus, will always be glad to have one of His own sweet words to go to sleep upon.

So here are thirty-one 'little pillows', not to be used all at once, nor even two at a time, but one for every night in the month. The little texts are so short, that they will need no learning; but when you have read the explanation, you will be able to keep the text quite safely and quite easily in your mind. Read the little book before you kneel down to say your evening prayers, because I hope what you read will always remind you of something to pray about. And then, when you lie down and shut your eyes, let your heart rest on the 'little pillow' till 'He giveth His beloved sleep'.

Frances told her little readers that when they had read the book, another would be ready for them entitled *Morning Bells*, describing it as 'little chimes of Bible music to wake them up'. 'Some of them', she wrote, 'will, I hope, ring in your ears all the day, and help you to go happily and brightly through it, following Jesus at every step'.

INSTRUMENTS

'Yield…your members as instruments of righteousness unto God'
(Romans 6:13)

This does not sound so easy and tuneful as most of your other 'morning bells', you think! But listen for a few minutes and you will hear the music.

What are your members? Hands, feet, lips, eyes, ears, and so on. What are you to do with them? 'Yield' them, that is, give them up altogether, hand them over to God.

What for? That He may use them as instruments of righteousness. That is, just as we should take an instrument of music, to make music with it, so He may take your hands and feet and all your members, and use them to do right and good things with.

If a little one gives himself or herself to God, every part of that little body is to be God's little servant, a little instrument for Him to use.

The little hands will no longer serve Satan by striking or pinching; the little feet will not kick or stamp, nor drag and dawdle, when they ought to run briskly on some errand; the little lips will not pout; the little tongue will not move to say a naughty thing. All the little members will leave off serving Satan, and find something to do for God; for if you 'yield' them to God, He will really take them and use them.

He will tell the hands to pick up what a tired mamma has dropped, and to fetch her a footstool; and the fingers to sew patiently at a warm petticoat for a poor child, or to make warm cuffs for a poor old man. He will tell the feet to run on errands of kindness and help. He will set the lips to sing happy hymns, which will cheer and comfort somebody, even if you never know of it. He will use the eyes for reading to some poor sick or blind woman, or to some fretful little one in your own home. You will be quite surprised to find in how many ways He will really use even your little members, if you give them and your whole self to Him. It will be so nice! You will never be miserable again with 'nothing to do'.

Take my hands, and let them move
At the impulse of Thy love.
Take my feet, and let them be
Swift and beautiful for Thee.

(Fifth Day of *Morning Bells*)

To the modern reader these words may sound somewhat 'quaint', but Frances knew of many to whom they were the 'words of life'. The books were enormously popular and sold in their thousands. In a letter to a friend she told how when she gave the manuscript to her publisher—Nisbet—they 'boldly started an edition of four thousand each, which were not in time for the advantage of Christmas orders!' However, within seven weeks a reprint was needed!

Frances did not find it nearly so easy to write for children as adults. Referring to these daily readings, she commented: 'constantly I refrained from what I would most like to say about the texts I had chosen, because it would not be simple enough for the little ones. I have purposely avoided any stories or anecdotes, lest children should skim the book through in search of them, instead of reading them morning and night steadily; at least I know that is what I should have done'.

In 1876 Frances heard from the Punjab that *Morning Bells* and *Little Pillows* were going to be translated into Hindustani and were already used in Mission schools. She also learnt that the Religious Tract Society of France was going to translate and publish them.

When Frances was staying with Mrs. Pennefather in Mildmay (as mentioned in chapter 7), she was taken to Clapton House, a Christian school for girls. On hearing that the Principal was not able to teach their Bible class, Frances offered to fill in. Afterwards she had a group of girls gathered in the drawing-room to talk further and said to them, 'Oh, don't sit all in a row a long way off; come up close and cosy; we can talk ever so much better then, can't we?' They were all charmed by this invitation and clustered around her in 'niece-fashion', enjoying a time of sharing questions and difficulties which was summed up by one of them, 'We do so want to come closer to Jesus'. Frances seemed to have such a way with her that she put everyone at ease when talking with them and drew out their confidence. We have seen that in other places in this book—in Ireland, Switzerland, on a boat or in a hotel—wherever she went she had the gift of conversation, proving to be good company but never losing an opportunity of talking of her King.

- A Move to Shareshill -

When the family left St. Nicholas Church in Worcester to go to Shareshill (a few miles from Wolverhampton), one of the hardest things for Frances to face was leaving her Sunday School class. The girls had become very dear to her despite many ups and downs, and she records that 'Often, when cold and lifeless in prayer, my nightly intercession for them has unsealed the frozen fountain, and the blessings sought for them seemed to fall on myself'.

In Worcester Frances had a neatly kept register entitled 'My Sunday School Scholars, from 1846 to 1860' with each child's details such as birthdays, anything of significance that occurred in their home, general impressions of their character etc. She freely admitted that though she might have a very sincere love and interest in other children, she would never be able to give any future class the same intensity of affection which these won and some reciprocated.

– Children's Books –

Another of Frances' books for children was called *Ben Brightboots*, the story being based on incidents involving the Shaw children, their tabby kitten and its offspring. The book also contained several other pieces and shows her skill in writing narrative as well as poetry and prose. We have included one of these stories entitled 'Arthur Phillips' in the chapter on 'Miscellaneous Papers'. The book was published posthumously in a very attractive format and was a best seller.

During the last months of her life, Frances was preparing a book for invalids, *Starlight Through the Shadows*, and had written eleven of the thirteen chapters she planned. But she felt constrained to break off and turn to writing another book for children. Sadly she died before she could return to the book for invalids, but it was published posthumously by her sister, Maria, who included some of her other writings 'to fill up the leaf withal'. The book for children that she was able to write was entitled *Morning Stars*, providing daily readings for a month. The difference with this book from her two previous ones, *Little Pillows* and *Morning Bells*, was that where the texts were quoted she inserted brackets to allow the readers to find the references for themselves, thus encouraging them to search the Scriptures. An excerpt from Day 2 is given here:

This name of the Lord Jesus ['I am...the Bright and Morning Star'] seems as if it must be meant especially for children, for it is those who get up early who see the beautiful morning star, shining in the quiet sky that is just beginning to be touched with a promise of dawn, and He says, 'those that seek Me early shall find Me' (Proverbs   ).

Jesus calls Himself the Bright Star, for He is the brightness of the Father's glory (Hebrews   )...You could not possibly have a dismal face while you are really 'looking unto Jesus' (Hebrews   ).

He calls Himself the Morning Star too...The sight of the morning star is the promise of the day. And so if you get a little glimpse by faith of the brightness of the Lord Jesus Christ now, it is only a beginning of clearer sight, and a pledge of the glorious day that has no night, in the land where you shall see the King in His beauty (Isaiah   ).

Frances lived as she wrote. Her written works very much reflected her life. Wherever she went the children that she met were special to her, and we have glimpses of her affection for her Sunday School class in Worcester, and for her nephews and nieces, some of whom she tutored in their own homes. Two of these nephews, William and Alfred, who were sons of Giles and Ellen Shaw, were the subject of a note written by Frances to her sisters Maria and Ellen:

> Rejoice with us—the first-fruits of the week [a mission held in Bewdley] are here, Willie—oh so rejoicing & decided, yesterday was indeed his spiritual birthday, he has so fully come to it & found joy...I hope Alf, too, but not so sure.

Another of her writings for children was entitled *Four Happy Days*. This was clearly autobiographical and is the story of a little girl called 'Annie' whose life mirrored Frances' own experience from her early days through to her conversion. In this piece we have an insight into her deep thoughts of sadness about her mother's death, but also her joy in realising that Jesus was her Saviour. She wanted children to know that, rather than just living for 'special or happy days,' such as birthdays etc., each day was given as a gift from God and would bring its own enjoyments and challenges.

Frances wrote many things to encourage her younger friends to read the Scriptures and apply what they learned to their own lives, as in the following piece:

'I SAY UNTO YOU'

For verily I say unto you, Till heaven and earth pass, one jot or one tittle shall in no wise pass from the law, till all be fulfilled.
(Matthew 5:18)

> See how many times these four little words come in to-day's and to-morrow's readings! [in the Children's Scripture Union, in connection with the Children's Special Service Mission] What the Lord Jesus said so often, we surely ought to notice.
>
> It makes all the difference who says a thing. If you could get near enough to the Queen to hear her say anything, you would listen with all your might. And if she began 'I say', you would lean forward to make sure of hearing what she had to say. But if she said, 'I say to you', I am sure no one would need to tell you to pay attention.

Now the Lord Jesus says, over and over again: 'I say unto you'. It was not only that He did say it a long time ago, but that whenever you look at the words He is saying it still. For His words are not dead; they are live words, just as much as if He had said them a minute ago. For He says, 'they are spirit and life', and that they shall 'never pass away'. So when you come to 'I say unto you', remember Jesus means it, and that He really means you to pay the same attention to what comes next as if He were speaking aloud to you.

And then remember it always means 'I say unto you'; not only the disciples who went up to Him in the mountain, but each of you who are just beginning to be one of His learners, for that is what 'disciple' means. Some of the things He says may be a little more than you can understand yet, but they are said to you all the same. When I was a little girl I had a sovereign given me. If it had been a shilling I might have put it in my own little purse, and spent it at once; but, being a sovereign, my dear father took care of it for me, and I expect I forgot all about it. But one day when I was quite grown up, he called me into his study and gave me the sovereign, reminding me how it had been given me when I was about as high as the back of a chair. And I was very glad to have it then, for I understood how much it was worth, and knew very well what to do with it. Now, when you come to some saying of the Lord Jesus that you do not understand or see how to make any use of for yourself, do not think it of no consequence whether you read it or not. When you are older you will find that it is just like my sovereign, coming back to you, when you want it and are able to make use of it. But how good it is of the Lord Jesus to have said so many things that are just what will help you now! Be on the look out for them every time you read, and see if you don't find something every day which is for you now. Ask for the Holy Spirit always before you begin, and then you may say as Habakkuk did, 'I will watch to see what He will say unto me'.

Suppose you keep a sharp-pointed pencil or a fine pen in the place where you usually read your Bible, and mark every time that the Lord Jesus says 'I say unto you'. And I think it would be a good plan if you put a double mark to every saying of His which you feel has come home to your own heart. You will remember them better, and it will help you to find them again.

(*Ben Brightboots*)

Such was the practical teaching Frances gave to her scholars.

The following verses were written by Frances and set to music by Alberto Randegger in *Sacred Songs for Little Singers*:

EVENING PRAYER

Now my evening praise I give;
Thou didst die that I might live,
All my blessings come from Thee,
Oh, how good Thou art to me.

Thou my best and kindest Friend;
Thou wilt love me to the end!
Let me love Thee more and more,
Always better than before.

(fourth and fifth verses; *Sacred Songs for Little Singers*)

Chapter Ten

A Beloved Father

There was a deep bond of love between Frances and her father: she was like him in many ways, and he had a strong influence on her life both in spiritual things and also in music. So perhaps it would be of interest to know a little of his background.

William Henry Havergal was born on January 18, 1793, the only son of William and Mary Havergal. There are few records of his early years—his only misdemeanour reported was that he took his cat to bed! He had a great love for animals and nature in general which he harboured to the end of his life.

When he was eight years old he was sent to a school in Princes Risborough, and this was his first letter home:

HONOURD PARENTS

I write these lines unto you hoping you are all well as it leaves me at present if you please to send me some almonds and raisins and fireworks I love my school very well we rise about Six and go to bed at eight give my best regards to Mrs. Shaw my duty to Grandfather and Grandmother. I received the two parcels safe which you sent and I thank you very much please to give my love to my sister I remain

Your dutiful Son
WILLIAM H HAVERGAL

P.S. by the Master: Accept my kind respects. It is necessary to say the above is Master William's own in every respect, as I make it a point never to alter the first production in any particular.

He subsequently went to Merchant Taylor's school in London and in the holidays cultivated music, practising on the piano and flute. From the age of fourteen he often played the organ in his parish church and composed several hymns for its anniversary occasions.

William Havergal went on to Oxford and gained a B.A. and later an M.A. Although he had an interest in medicine before going to university—which proved valuable later in his visiting ministry—he knew he must read theology. He was subsequently ordained in 1816 in Wells Cathedral. Also in 1816 he married Jane Head, daughter of William and Mary Head of East Grinstead.

After two curacies, the first at St. James, Bristol and the second at Coaley in Gloucestershire, Havergal was appointed curate of Astley Church, Worcester, in 1822. As the rector was an invalid, W.H.H. was virtually in charge of the parish, and from the first was able to take up residence at the rectory with his family. In 1829 he was offered the living, and so by the time Frances was born Astley rectory had been the family home for 14 years. We have seen something of Frances' early years there as related in chapter one.

– A Move to Worcester –

The family left Astley in 1842, and after a temporary home nearby at Henwick House, they moved to Worcester when W.H.H. was appointed rector of St. Nicholas Church. Not only was Mr. Havergal's preaching to prove a great blessing to his flock, but he was also much appreciated for his pastoral visitation to the old and the young. Many of the poor of Worcester bore testimony to his great kindness, always ready to give a helping hand to those who were in need. A retired tradesman, who formerly never frequented the church, spoke of him thus: 'Ah, nobody preaches like Mr. Havergal; he teaches me what I want. I tell you what he does: he takes a text, picks it all to pieces, and shows us what is inside it, and then makes us feel it'.

A little girl, Emma, in the Sunday School, who was very ill, would watch for his quick step, and longed for the time of his visits to come. She especially prized his Sunday evening visits on his way home from preaching at St. Nicholas. Once, when he was sent for after church to another invalid, she would not go to bed, but lay watching for him till after ten o'clock, knowing he never forgot to come. He had always taken a special interest in the children of the parish, but when he first came to St. Nicholas' there was no single centre for their education. A day school was in existence, but it was scattered over a wide area in small teaching units, and he felt this to be very unsatisfactory.

One morning an early rap at his study door announced Mr. John Wheeley Lea, partner in the Lea & Perrins Company, whose business included the manufacture of Lea & Perrins Worcester sauce; he had come to inform Mr. Havergal that it was a jubilee-day with him. For fifty years God had prospered him commercially, and now he had come to propose a thanksgiving offering, and he also wanted to show his appreciation of Mr. Havergal's ministry. When told he was to choose how this was to be done, the pastor replied: 'Schools! Schools!' A borrowed room on Sunday, and a wide scattering of the children on weekdays, had long been a grief to him, and this was a true answer to prayer. The jubilee schools were accordingly built to cater for 160 children at a cost of over £1,000. Some years later several comfortable almshouses were also built by Mr. Lea.

- A Serious Accident -

On the 14th of June, 1829 Havergal met with a distressing and almost fatal accident. He was driving alone to fetch his eldest daughter from school near Worcester, when the usually steady horse suddenly swerved, throwing him out of the carriage, and causing a serious concussion. He was prevented from his clerical duties for some time, and his vision was affected for the rest of his life. During the time of convalescence his studious and active mind found relief in music, devoting much or nearly all of his royalties for published music to the Church Missionary Society and occasionally to other ministries.

- Missionary Work -

W.H.H. was an early advocate of support for the Church Missionary Society, and he travelled to many churches in the U.K. over several decades to present the work of the Society and to raise awareness of the needs of the workers overseas. No doubt the lively stories he had to tell of missionary adventures when he returned from these tours fired his youngest daughter's imagination as she listened intently to what he told the family. So much so that she first became a collector for missionary work when she was a small child, and the joy of giving thus stayed with her throughout her life. She gave very generously and sacrificially to foreign missions. She also used her artistic and poetic gifts to produce cards for special occasions, or to enclose in letters, and these sold in their thousands. The money raised from these and from much of her published works she gladly gave to missionary work. She would have joined her very close friend Elizabeth Clay in India if her health had been strong enough to let her do so, but as she was prevented from doing that, she felt it was her privilege to do all she could to support the missionaries on the field.

– Musical Gifts –

William Henry Havergal was very gifted musically and had been offered a professorship in music at Oxford University, but he declined because he knew his first calling was to the gospel ministry. He was regarded as the foremost church musician and composer of sacred music in England in his generation. He used his gifts in music (as a fine organist, choir master, and composer) as a help in his pastoral work, and also as a pleasure when he was tired or incapacitated by health from full-time work. He was undoubtedly a fine composer (the winner of two Gresham prizes, after which the judges concluded not to grant a third prize to a composer) and also wrote on historical matters in music.

He made it clear, though, that he preferred to write a sermon rather than a music score! A look into his study and on his bookshelves would have revealed what good company he kept! Calvin's works stood side by side with the works of Pearson and Hooker, Jeremy Taylor and many Puritan divines, as well as the commentaries of Scott and Matthew Henry.

– Move to Shareshill –

Because of the debilitating effects of his accident he did not feel he could truly fulfil all his responsibilities in a busy city parish. So when in 1859 he received the offer of the very small rural living of Shareshill in the diocese of Lichfield, he accepted it gratefully and went there in March 1860.

In an article published in *The Christian* periodical on December 31, 1936 entitled 'The Home of the Havergals,' the Rev. Lewis H. Court told of his visit to the hamlet of Share's Hill (as he described it). There he met those who testified of the great blessing resulting from W.H.H.'s preaching, and that it had a great effect upon his parishioners.

> Rectory as well as church kept an open door for God's poor; and on New Year's Day the aged poor of the parish were given a dinner at the rectory, after which the pastor and his daughters would sing and play to entertain them; and he would give them a spiritual address which would inspire and comfort them. Gifts of helpful books and comforters brought these parties to a close.

'Thanks for all favours for all blessings on their dear pastor' were then voiced by old George Adams—a man whose conversion from a rather dissolute manner of life made him a bright witness to his neighbours of the power of redeeming grace.

In 1866 Frances returned to Shareshill from Oakhampton, where she had been staying with her sister Miriam, and her work in the young women's Bible class at the rectory evidently made an indelible impression on the minds of her scholars—a few of whom still remained to recall to Mr. Court what manner of woman she was. Her beautiful eyes, as one of them told him, 'were enough to rebuke the least delinquency on our part, without any single word of reproof'.

– *Retirement and 'an abundant entrance'* –

Later in 1866 it was felt that, due to failing health, William Havergal should retire from active work, so in 1867 he bought a house in Leamington and called it Pyrmont Villa after his favourite resort in Germany. This was his last home, but he was able to return to Pyrmont and take Sunday services for the English visitors in 1869. It was here in Leamington that he resided until his death on April 19th, 1870.

Many pictures could be drawn of Frances' home life in Leamington. She especially valued the sympathy of her father in all her studies.

She delighted to talk out hard questions with him, and his classical knowledge, as well as his poetic and musical skill, settled many a point. She would rush down with her new poems or thoughts, awaiting his criticisms. And she loved to accompany him when he would sing his hymns. Her sister Maria wrote of him and Frances, '...I have seen her absorbed with his improvised melodies, fugues and intricate progressions, thrilling yet passing. His holy and consistent example, ever holding forth the word of life and sound doctrine, has been a guiding light on his child's path'.

So we can understand why his sudden death in 1870 left a sorrowful blank in the home in Leamington for Frances because she would no longer have his help in her writings and music, or know his fatherly love for her. Writing to a friend later that year she wrote:

> Home life is very different, and in spite of my pleasant work, very sad. No one guesses how much I miss dear Papa, because I can flash up and talk and laugh when spoken to, and people (Mamma included) think, of course, that, because I can do so, I do not feel it much. But God knows how intensely I miss him, and how desolate and fatherless I do feel, and how there are no smiles, but often enough tears, when I am quite alone.

Those who knew Mr. Havergal spoke well of him, saying that he was no ordinary man. He was rich in grace as well as gifts. 'Who could see him and not love him?' asked a fellow pastor, his friend for many years. His daughter Miriam wrote a biography, *Records of the Life of the Rev. William Henry Havergal M.A.*, and a notice in the Oldham Chronicle drew the conclusion that it 'deserves to take its place with the *Memoirs* of M'Cheyne. It has the same gracious interest, the same powerful unction, the same fervour, force, tender love and practical sympathy...It is a biographical gem, and deserves a place in every Christian home.'

Very late in her life, Maria gave a collection of important artifacts belonging to her father, and sister Frances, to the Church Missionary Society, a deposit now located in the C.M.S. archives at the University of Birmingham (England). Among such items is a small book William Henry kept for decades, recording his sermons with the texts and the locations preached. Those recorded begin with one preached March 31, 1816 in Durston on Acts 4:12, and the last recorded one preached on January 3, 1869 at Pyrmont [Germany] on Deuteronomy 33:16.

These words are written in Maria's hand on the cover of the small Volume mentioned above:

Rev. W.H. Havergal's life prints.
'A faithful minister in the Lord'. –
The Record of texts &
Sermons—from March 31, 1816,
to Janry 3.1869. Sermons from
June 5. to Sept. 12. 1869 not entered.
The last text "The Lord Jesus Christ be
with thy spirit". Preached at Pyrmont—(illegible word)
Sept. 1869. Bequeathed to the
C.M.S. 1886. M.V.G.H.

'MY TIMES ARE IN THY HAND.'

My times are in Thy hand,
Their best and fittest place,
I would not have them at command
Without Thy guiding grace.

'My times', and yet not mine, –
I could not them ordain;
Not one e'er waits from me a sign,
Nor can I one detain.

'My times', O Lord, are Thine,
And Thine their oversight:
Thy wisdom, love and power combine
To make them dark or bright.

I know not what shall be,
When passing times are fled;
But all events I leave with Thee,
And calmly bow my head.

Hence, Lord, in Thee I rest,
And wait Thy holy will;
I lean upon my Saviour's breast
Or gladly go on still.

And when 'my times' shall cease,
And life shall fade away,
Then bid me, Lord, depart in peace
To realms of endless day!

William Henry Havergal

Chapter Eleven

Miscellaneous Papers

Such was the wealth of material on Frances Ridley Havergal made available to me by the researcher of all Havergal's works, that this book is but the tip of the iceberg. In this chapter some of her writings have been chosen to demonstrate her gifts of poetry, prose and narrative, as well as to show her love and care for others in their physical and temporal needs, and more importantly, how she sought to show them the provision of God in Christ.

Although Frances was in her early teens when Captain Allan Gardiner, the founder of the Patagonian Mission, died, she was obviously deeply affected by his death and put her thoughts into the poem quoted below. Allan Gardiner (born 1794) was a sea-faring man serving in the Royal Navy for a number of years. But his heart's desire was to take the gospel to those in distant lands whom he had seen on his travels, and so he resigned his captaincy and went out to South America. There he endured much hardship and suffering during his missionary endeavours, and in 1851 finally succumbed to a lonely death while seeking to open up the southern tip of South America to the gospel. Just before he died, unable to move and with no strength, Gardiner wrote:

> Blessed be my heavenly Father for the many mercies I enjoy: a comfortable bed, no pain or cravings for hunger, though excessively weak, scarcely able to turn in my bed, at least it is a very great exertion; but I am, by His abounding grace, kept in perfect peace, refreshed with a sense of my Saviour's love and an assurance that all is wisely and mercifully appointed.

His body was found four months later when a ship passed by where he lay. But his faith in God evidently remained steadfast to the end. Frances wrote this poem in 1852, when she was fifteen.

ON THE DEATH OF CAPTAIN ALLAN GARDINER
The First Missionary to Patagonia

In desolate wild grandeur all around,
　Dark rocky spires are tow'ring to the sky,
　While through the caverns echoes far the sound
Of winds, which o'er Antarctic seas sweep fitfully.

The ocean waves with deep and hollow tone
　Combat the haughty cliffs in fierce affray,
　Then back returning with a sullen moan,
Sink, till again they dash, their warrior spray.

No flowerets spring that barren land to cheer,
　No waving trees salute that stormy sky
　With graceful bend; scarce grass and herbs appear,
Or aught of greenery, to soothe the weary eye.

O who in such a dreary clime could dwell?
　Who would abide on such a desert shore?
　Save the wild native, who, our sailors tell,
No Saviour know, no Deity supreme adore.

But list awhile! Who breathed that deep-drawn sigh?
　Whence came it? Hark again! A voice of prayer,
　Mingled with heavenly praises, rose on high,
As with sweet incense hallowing the chilly air.

Alone, no earthly friend or brother near,
　A human form lies on that bleak, bleak strand.
　Sunken his eye, and wan his cheeks appear,
For famine pall has laid on him her withering hand.

No food nor water six long weary days
　Have passed those pallid lips, yet not a plaint
　From him may fall, but notes of joyful praise;
Sustained with bread of life his soul can never faint.

For Jesus whispers comfort to his soul,
  And smooths his pillow, though so cold and hard;
He hears no wind, he sees no surges roll,
He only hears his Master, sees his bright reward.

Another sigh, his happy soul hath flown
  From its frail dwelling, where so long it lay
Pinioned, his painful toils at length are done,
And angels welcome him to dwell in endless day.

Wherefore left he his lovely native isle?
  Wherefore his life, his all thus sacrifice?
Did he for pleasure undertake such toil?
Was it for sordid gold, which men so highly prize?

No, higher motive filled that noble breast;
  He sacrificed his all from Christian love,
He went to tell of peace and heavenly rest,
To teach those heathen of a gracious God above.

And shall we blame him, who devoted thus
  To his great Master's name his freshest days?
Despise that bright example left to us,
And on his memory strive to cast a gloomy haze?

Shame, shame on those who dare aspersions fling
  On Gardiner's honoured name! They know it's true
Right well he served his Saviour and his King;
And they who love the Master, love the servant too.

But now he rests in peace, his labours past;
  Nothing can vex that noble spirit more,
For he hath gained his distant port at last,
The waves have only carried him to that blest shore.

No laurels bloomed on that pale dying brow
  No earthly honours clustered round that bed;
But victor–wreaths encircle now,
And a bright crown adorns that mission martyr's head!

(*The Complete Poetical Works of Frances Ridley Havergal*)

Frances was eager to express her thoughts of Gardiner's total dedication to his Master and his great desire to evangelise part of South America in spite of some who were not altogether in agreement with his endeavours. His sacrifice was not in vain, however, as people at home, greatly moved by his death, purchased a schooner, and named it the *Allan Gardiner*. It was used to take the gospel to the aboriginals of South America. Later the Lord blessed the work, and many lost people, so notorious for their savage ways, became true followers of Christ, a bright testimony of His saving grace.

* * * * * *

In September 1878 Frances gave an address to the Young Women's Christian Association in Plymouth on 'All Things'. While there she probably heard of Agnes Weston's work among the sailors, called the 'Royal Sailors' Rests', which was founded in 1876. This obviously captured her imagination and she was eager to pass on the following story to challenge her younger readers. After Frances' unexpected death in 1879, her sister Maria published this as part of the book for children, *Ben Brightboots and Other True Stories*, *Hymns, and Music* by F.R.H.

THE STORY OF ARTHUR PHILLIPS

"Therefore be ye also ready."
(Matthew 24:44)

I wonder if you have heard of Miss Weston, and the good work she is doing among the sailors, and the interesting book she has written about them, called "Our Blue-jackets"? I will tell you about one of her Blue jackets, Arthur Phillips, and how she came to know him.

She was staying with a friend at Plymouth, a place where there are a great many ships and sailors. And she saw that on Sunday afternoons there were numbers of sailor boys wandering about the streets, with no friends, and no place to go to, and nothing to do; so that it was no wonder if they got into bad company. She felt very sorry for them, and thought perhaps some of them had good mothers praying for them in some far away home, and how troubled they must be when they thought of their boys with no one to care for them. So she set to work to see what she could do for them. She sent little notices to all the ships that the boys might come and meet her in a large room for singing and reading on Sunday afternoons. But an officer told her he was afraid it would be of no use; he said, "they are as restless when they come ashore as birds let out of a cage." And so, sure enough, after waiting two hours the first Sunday, only one lad came, and he was too frightened to stay all alone.

The next Sunday not one came, nor the next, nor the next. And then most persons would have said, "Oh, it's no use!" and given it up. But Miss Weston did not say that; she did the best thing anybody possibly can do when they are disappointed and puzzled, she "went and told Jesus" all about it. He knew how much she wanted to help these poor lads, and so He showed her another way to catch them.

The friend with whom she was staying offered the use of her kitchen for them, with tea and cake into the bargain. Then two good men offered to go out into the streets and try to bring them in. Very soon a dozen came, and they liked the tea and cake and cosy warm kitchen so much that they brought others, and then there were two dozen, and then three dozen, and they sat on the window ledge, and among the cups and saucers on the dresser, and even inside the grate, till before long the kitchen could not hold them at all.

It was not only for cake and tea that they came; they sang hymns and listened to their friend as she told them Bible stories and prayed with them. So the officer was wrong after all; perhaps he did not know how the story of the love of Jesus can make a restless sailor boy listen. Jesus said, "I, if I be lifted up, will draw all men unto Me," and you see how this came true, and even these wild lads, let loose from their ships, were drawn when He was lifted up among them.

Among those whom Jesus really drew to Himself was a fine young sailor named Arthur Phillips. Sunday after Sunday he was always at the meeting. As regularly as the clock struck three, he might be seen with his happy sunburnt face, coming up the garden path, bringing two or three others with him. When the kitchen got too full he would say, "Well, we are crowded out; we shall soon have to ask God to give us a larger place, Miss Weston." One Sunday he brought the news that he was going away to sea. It was his last meeting, and the tears were in his eyes as he said good-bye with the words: "Never mind: it is God's will; my Saviour will be with me. And as soon as we come into Plymouth sound again I shall be up at these dear old meetings like a shot."

And so Arthur went to sea. He was so happy and bright, that, although he was so young, the rough sailors could not help feeling his influence; his little lamp was kept burning so clear that it made a light in a dark place. It shows what influence one who is shining for Jesus may have, that very often a wicked man would stop swearing if he noticed that Arthur was near. The secret of his brightness was his keeping near to Jesus. If you really love any one, you are sure to try to go and be with them when you can. So as Arthur loved his Saviour he wanted to be alone with him when he could, and yet that cannot be very easy on board a ship; not nearly so easy as it is for you to get away upstairs and have a nice little quiet time by your bedside. But where there's a will there's a way, and so every day, during the dinner hour, Arthur used to run down a ladder into a place called the "bag-racks," that he might be a little while alone with Jesus. I expect it must have been very dark down there, but he would not mind that.

One day he tripped down the ladder as usual. There was an open hatchway just below; perhaps he slipped, perhaps it was too dark to see, we can never know how it was, but he fell, and in an instant Arthur was in glory. No bones broken, no marks on his body, no time for any pain at all!

Was it not beautiful! going happily down to pray to his beloved Lord in the dark, and all at once finding himself in the light of His presence caught away to be with Jesus for ever! It was "sudden death, sudden glory." Would sudden death be sudden glory to you?

(*Ben Brightboots*)

*   *   *   *   *   *

Frances was often found visiting the poor folk in the almshouses, cottages and infirmary when she lived in Astley and was eager to do anything to improve their lot. She was an excellent seamstress and very innovative and while she was in Switzerland she made the following discovery:

HOW TO KEEP OURSELVES WARM

Although the Swiss peasants are what we should consider very poor, working very hard and earning very little; doing without many little comforts which are almost necessities in an English cottage, and dressing at less cost than our own cottagers; one hardly ever hears of any real poverty or suffering from want or cold, yet their winters are far longer and more severe than ours. In the valley from which I write this (September), the snow lies from November until April.

One of their contrivances for winter warmth is so very simple that it might surely add to the comfort of many an English cottage, where there are many little ones to be kept warm at night and not many warm blankets or counterpanes to cover them. It is a hay quilt; and as I have several times slept cosily under one of them, on cold nights among the mountains, I can tell from experience how comfortable they are.

They are nothing but a large square cotton bag, with a few good handfuls of hay, shaken lightly into it; but they are as warm as two or three thick blankets. They need cost almost nothing. The breadths of a very old cotton dress run together, or old curtains, or any other used-out or washed-out material will do for the large double squares, which should be quite as wide as the bed which it is intended to cover. Any farmer would give a few handfuls of hay to shake into it; and there is a coverlet which will keep out any amount of cold! A Hay Quilt Working Party would in one afternoon provide almost as much comfort as an expensive Blanket fund. Or poor mothers might themselves, with little trouble and less expense, make their little children or aged parents nice and warm at night, if they would only try this simple plan of the poor Swiss mountaineers.

(published in an unknown periodical)

In our day they are known as duvets or comforters!

* * * * * *

A few months after the death of her father, whom she still missed intensely, Frances was obviously being encouraged by the letters she had received about the hymns she composed for *Songs of Grace and Glory*, and in October 1870 wrote in answer to a friend's communication:

It does seem wonderful that God should so use and bless my hymns; and yet it really does seem as if the seal of His own blessing were set upon them, for so many testimonials have reached me. Writing is praying with me, for I never seem to write even a verse by myself, and feel like a little child writing; you know a child would look up at every sentence and say, 'And what shall I say next?' That is just what I do; I ask that every line He would give me, not merely thoughts and power, but also every word, even the very rhymes.

Frances wrote to a friend in 1878:

Parlane [who published some of her leaflets] sent me some time ago a letter from the widow of good Duncan Matheson. He had owed P. about £20 for printing his hymn book. Mrs. Matheson paid it, and Parlane generously returned the whole to her. She says: 'When you sent the account, it came the day after my beloved husband died. You enclosed a leaflet by F.R.H., the text at the heading was, "My God shall

all your need supply". I cannot tell you the blessing I got in reading it, and each day it has been in my mind, and I have felt its sweetness, and now your returning the money is another proof of His faithfulness'. I am so glad I had thus unwittingly the privilege of comforting Duncan Matheson's widow.

This is the poem mentioned in the letter:

GOD THE PROVIDER

'My God shall supply all your need, according to
His riches in glory by Christ Jesus.'
(Philippians 4:19)

Who shall tell our untold need,
　　Deeply felt, though scarcely known!
Who the hungering soul can feed,
　　Guard, and guide, but God alone?
Blessed promise! While we see
Earthly friends must powerless be,
Earthly fountains quickly dry:
'*God*' shall all your need supply.

He hath said it! So we know
　　Nothing less can we receive.
Oh that thankful love may glow
　　While we restfully believe, -
Ask not how, but trust Him still;
Ask not when, but wait His will:
Simply on His word rely,
God '*shall*' all your need supply.

Through the whole of life's long way,
　　Outward, inward need we trace;
Need arising day by day,
　　Patience, wisdom, strength, and grace.
Needing Jesus most of all,
Full of need, on Him we call;
Then how gracious His reply,
God shall '*all*' your need supply.

Great our need, but greater far
　　Is our Father's loving power;
He upholds each mighty star,
　　He unfolds each tiny flower.

He who numbers every hair,
Earnest of His faithful care,
Gave His Son for us to die;
God shall all '*your*' need supply.

Yet we often vainly plead
    For a fancied good denied,
What we deemed a pressing need
    Still remaining unsupplied.
Yet from dangers all concealed,
Thus our wisest Friend doth shield;
No good thing will He deny,
God shall all your '*need*' supply.

Can we count redemption's treasure,
    Scan the glory of God's love?
Such shall be the boundless measure
    Of His blessings from above.
All we ask or think, and more,
He will give in bounteous store, -
He can fill and satisfy!
God shall all your need '*supply*'.*

One the channel, deep and broad,
    From the Fountain of the Throne,
Christ the Saviour, Son of God,
    Blessings flow through Him alone.
He, the Faithful and the True,
Brings us mercies ever new:
Till we reach His home on high,
'*God shall all your need supply*'.

*The Greek word is much stronger than the English,—'will supply to the full', 'fill up', 'satisfy'.

(*The Ministry of Song*)

On another occasion she wrote to a young man who was planning to enter the ministry:

I have enclosed a parcel for you. It is a present which you won't care twopence for at present, so you needn't profess to! But I believe you will care for it if, please God, this time ten years or so, you are bringing forth out of His treasure things new and old for some flock committed to you. It is a set of Goodwin's *Works*—one of the grandest and oldest of the 17th century writers—much too deep and solid for modern taste, but full of Christ and of 'the deep things of God'. Some day if you are going to preach out of Ephesians, you will find, I should think, everything that could be said on every single word of the first, and part of the second chapter. He is called 'that peerless divine, and star of the first magnitude'!

* * * * * *

After Frances died, her niece and god-daughter (Frances Anna Shaw 1856–1948), compiled a small collection of previously never published letters and Bible notes by F.R.H., a Thirty-One Day book of morning and evening sections called *Treasure Trove*. Morning sections were taken from unpublished letters, and most of the evening sections were taken from notes in F.R.H.'s Bible. Between the title page and the preface of this book, the following poem was printed:

O Jesus Christ, my Master,
　I come to Thee today;
I ask Thee to direct me
　In all I do or say.
I want to keep my promise,
　To be Thy servant true;
I come to Thee for orders,
　Dear Lord, what shall I do?
I want a heart not heeding
　What others think or say;
I want an humble spirit
　To listen and obey.
To serve Thee without ceasing,
　'Tis but a little while,
My strength, the Master's promise;
　My joy, the Master's smile.
O precious Lord and Master,
　I want to hear Thy voice,
Enduing me with power
　And bidding me rejoice;

That while Thou still dost tarry,
I faithful may be found;
With lamp all trimmed and burning,
I wait the trumpet's sound.

(*Treasure Trove*)

These words sum up very powerfully the whole desire and longing of her heart. She had known much severe illness and many trials, but her faith burned brightly and she was ever looking and longing for the Lord's coming.

'Where your treasure is, there will your heart be also.'
(Luke 12:34)

Chapter Twelve

Frances and Her Music

Frances grew up in a very musical home. As we have seen in chapter ten, her father was a fine musician and all his six children were well-trained in music. When a baby, before she could sing or speak, Frances would 'coo' on the beat when her family would sing. As she grew up her true talent was developed and she could play piano music by Haydn, Mozart, Beethoven, Mendelssohn and others at great length from memory. Later in her life, while in Switzerland, Frances played a piano Sonata by Beethoven; an elderly lady in attendance had heard Beethoven himself play decades earlier, and she came up afterwards to say that Frances' playing reminded her much of Beethoven's own playing.

In 1865 her German friends encouraged her to visit Dr. Hiller in Cologne. Ferdinand Hiller was one of the leading musicians of his day—a close colleague and friend of Mendelssohn and a musician highly respected by Schumann, Chopin, Liszt and others. He was himself a fine pianist, composer and conductor. When Ferdinand Hiller met Frances and sight-read her manuscript scores, he was deeply impressed with her harmony and had difficulty believing that she had no academic training, and was largely self-taught, with only informal guidance in harmony and composition from her father.

In a letter written to a friend in 1866 Frances wrote:

How I should like to teach you harmony! I do believe I could make it lucid; you can't think what exquisite symmetry there is in chords and intervals, so that I always feel, as well as believe, that man by no means invented harmony, but only found out God's beautiful arrangements in it…I certainly do feel I have at least some sort of inherited instinct for seeing into harmonies. The way I studied harmonies was rather unique; some years ago (at home) I kept a treatise on harmony in my bedroom, read as much as I could conveniently grasp the last thing, and then worked out the exercises in my head before going to sleep.

– *Songs of Grace and Glory* –

This gift of harmony certainly proved to be very useful, not only in her composition of hymn tunes, but also in the work which she was to undertake for her father. When elderly, he asked Frances to proof and correct his latest compositions, and it was soon after his death in 1870 that she undertook the preparation for the press of *Havergal's Psalmody* and *Century of Chants*. This was her father's music with a few pieces composed by her. This book was the companion volume and the source of music scores for a new hymnbook, *Songs of Grace and Glory*, prepared by the Rev. Charles B. Snepp, minister and hymnologist, in collaboration with Frances as music editor. Mr. Snepp chose all the texts and was the architect of the structure; Frances prepared all the music which was an enormous body of work, involving countless hours over a number of years.

Late in 1870 she wrote of difficulties in the work:

I was so struck this morning with 'Thou art the Helper of the fatherless',—the very first time one of those special orphan promises has come home to me. I had been puzzling over a tune which papa would have decided about in a minute, and missed him so much, when suddenly this verse flashed upon me brightly. I think that even in music the Lord is my helper now; much more in other things.

Mr. Snepp commented:

In assisting me to carry out, through the press, this great work [the production of *Songs of Grace and Glory*], we had many difficulties, but also many answers to prayer. On more occasions than one, when the proof sheets were waiting, and the next hymn, upon some important and difficult subject, had scarcely reached the high standard desired, we paused for prayer, and, spreading the matter before the Lord, asked for His Divine Spirit to guide her pen; and, ere a brief hour or so had passed away, the much needed guidance was vouchsafed.

The work involved restoring the hymns to their originals, discovering authors' names and dates, selecting texts and tunes, and arranging more than a thousand hymns under their proper themes and subjects.

The British Library in London has a copy of the music edition of this hymnal published by James Nisbet & Co., London, 1883, 'Three Hundred and Thirteenth Thousand' for the printing number on the title page! But copies are now extremely rare.

Testimonies, from churches and missionaries, poured in from all parts speaking of the spiritual help and blessing received through this first edition. Letters from India, Australia and America tell of the great refreshment received, and New Zealand, Cape Town and the Holy Land could also speak of the same.

- The Tonic Sol-Fa -

This next piece was found in a cut-out clipping, though the name of the periodical was not given. The date, October 15, 1870, was printed at the top of the article.

October 15, 1870.

THE PHILANTHROPIC ASPECT OF THE TONIC SOL-FA MOVEMENT

A paper read, September 27th, 1870, before the social science Congress at Newcastle–on–Tyne, BY JOHN SPENCER CURWEN.

Of labour in another sphere the following lead from Miss Havergal speaks:

During the winter months we opened two rooms every evening, and gave free invitations to young dress-makers and girls of that class (especially those living in lodgings), hoping that it would prove a safe and pleasant retreat for them after work hard. Classes were arranged for each evening in the smaller room, in the other the girls read, wrote, worked and chatted. It was not as successful as to numbers as we expected, but the attendance on the evening in which I gave a Tonic Sol-fa lesson, was nearly double. I tell you frankly that it was not for the sake of Sol-fa that I began the class, but solely because I believed it was the greatest attraction I could contribute to our little scheme for bringing these poor girls within the range of loving Christian care and influence. My chief reason for adopting it with them instead of the established notation was that all the Sol-fa systems are sound and safe, and I knew I could not give them access to anything low or bad through it, while I had no such certainty had I taught the old notes. This weighed with me more than the obvious and indisputable advantages of greater facility, cheapness, etc. which the Tonic sol-fa system has. There was no question as to the class being attractive, and gone was the disappointment when, as frequently happened, the members were kept at work too late and 'missed the singing'. One evening, two girls came in paniced (sic) and flushed, about fifteen minutes before the class. 'Why Lizzie and Jane what is the matter?' 'We were kept overtime, but we thought half a loaf better than no bread, so we took to our heels the moment we could get out of the workroom, and we never stopped running till we got here'. They had literally run a good mile to be on time for a few minutes of singing. One young girl who had just begun to make acquaintances which would have led to no good began to saunter about the streets with them, was attracted to our rooms solely by the singing class, but soon became one of our most regular attendants at all the classes, and we have reason to hope that she is not only saved from the dangers into which she was running, but that good impressions have been made and a good work begun in her heart. I have no musical results to show, for after about eight lessons I was interrupted by illness, but I believe that my Tonic Sol-fa class had been a grappling iron to draw many little drifting vessels close to our side, bring them within hearing of loving and sympathising words and of the One name which is 'sweeter than any music'.

This account demonstrated that Frances' love for young people ever made her look out for opportunities to help them and lead them into the ways of truth. Music was, for her, a rich means to glorify her Saviour and to benefit others.

– *Loyal Responses with Music: Work for 1879: 'If the Lord will'* –

One of the tasks that Frances hoped to do in 1879 was to set her little book *Loyal Responses* to music. Her music publisher, Hutchings and Romer, had asked her to do this and her reply was 'I have so many irons in the fire, that I can barely find time to heat a musical one'. She had written some of the scores in pencil for these poems, but died before she could finish them. Her sister Maria later prepared the book to be finished, using some of Frances' other compositions for those poems that had not been set to music, and it was published posthumously as *Loyal Responses, The Last Melodies of Frances Ridley Havergal, With Other Poems and Tunes*. In the 'Prefatory Note' to this book Maria quoted F.R.H..'s statement on the subject of SACRED SONG:

> I am delighted to have an opportunity of adding to the very meagre supply of Sacred Songs, and I hope they will be sufficiently tuneful and sufficiently easy for drawing-room singing. Some of those extant are such pathetic and dismal affairs! Why put off joyous singing till we reach the happier shore? Let us sing words which we feel and love, with clearness of enunciation, and looking up to meet His smile all the while we are singing. So shall we loyally sing for our King, yes for Him, whose voice is our truest music.

– Excerpts on Music –

Included in the Appendix of *Memorials* are some of Frances' thoughts on music. She called music 'the only universal language, a sort of alphabet of the language of heaven'.

> To me the overture to the Lobgesang [the Symphony No. 2 in B-flat Major, Opus 52 by Felix Mendelssohn] is a vision of Christian life, with its own peculiar struggles and sorrows as well as joys. It is the sixth, seventh, and eighth chapters of the Epistle to the Romans in essence. The mingling of twilight yearnings, ever pressing onward, with calm and trustful praise, ever pressing upward, is an almost unbearably true echo of the heart, especially in the 6/8 Allegretto agitato; then the Andante religioso is the still, mellow glow of 'light at eventide', to which one looks forward; then I go just one step farther, and find a fore-echo of the eternal song in the burst of vocal praise, after the long tension of the voiceless overture.

> Is not the tendency of the human voice to fall from the true pitch, one of the results of 'the Fall'? Adam and Eve must have sung in tune, like the birds. How wonderful it is, that the birds not only sing their own songs in tune, but all the songs always seem in tune with each other, except the cuckoo, when passing from his major third in May to his minor third (or even second) in June!

May not one apply this to the dissonances within, that stun and bewilder and weary us, and believe that if we are indeed God's chosen praise-harps, all that is not as yet *tune* is but the *tuning*, which is *not* in itself beautiful.

Gregorians [chants] are to me only curious and interesting, like dried plants or fossils, not living and lovely.

Of the chorus 'And the glory of the Lord' (Handel's '*Messiah*') I shall never forget the impression of its first bars at the Birmingham Festival, 1867; it gave such a sense of clear sunny grandeur, massive open-browed stateliness, and fearless, glorious, overwhelmingness; a musical expression of one's ideal personification of TRUTH, majestically going forth conquering and to conquer.

Beethoven's 95th Psalm is a grandly jubilant thing, with contrasts of sternness and melancholy.

The magnificent massive choruses in the 'Israel in Egypt' need a gigantic orchestra to give scope for their great swing of grandeur. The mighty flinging of sound from side to side, in some of the double choruses, is what might be carried out if Handel had Salisbury Plain for his concert room, cannon for his basses, an army for his tenors, and angelic legions for his sopranos.

These are only glimpses of Frances' skills in music. She was a gifted pianist and could sing beautifully, effectively reaching her hearers' minds and hearts, as well as being a fine composer. Her poetry and prose are now known, but few today realize how important her musical gifts were in her life and work.

THE MOONLIGHT SONATA
Introduction

The ills we see,—
The mysteries of sorrow deep and long,
The dark enigmas of permitted wrong,—
Have all one key:
This strange, sad world is but our Father's school;
All chance and change His love shall grandly overrule.

How sweet to know
The trials which we cannot comprehend
Have each their own divinely-purposed end!
He traineth so
For higher learning, ever onward reaching
For fuller knowledge yet, and His own deeper teaching.

(first and second stanzas; *Under the Surface*)

Chapter Thirteen

'To Live Well is Good: To Die Well is Better'

'For so an entrance shall be ministered unto you
abundantly into the everlasting kingdom of our
Lord and Saviour Jesus Christ.'
(2 Peter 1:11)

In the latter part of 1874, Frances Havergal developed a fever while in Switzerland. She managed to return home and went to stay with her sister Ellen at Winterdyne. At one point it seemed life-threatening, but after a few months of rest and recuperation she was restored, though there were further periods of severe illness. However, with the return of health came a return to work until 1879.

After Frances' father died in April 1870, she spent much of the next eight years attending to her stepmother, Caroline (Cooke) Havergal. When Mrs. Havergal died in May 1878 this necessitated the breakup of their Leamington home. It involved much hard work and many decisions: a lifetime's accumulation of family possessions had to be sorted and disposed of, and what Maria and Frances salvaged for themselves had to be reduced to fit into a furnished accommodation. Frances concentrated on the tools of her trade—desk, table, books, an American typewriter, a favourite chair from Astley days, and her harp piano with its stand which 'she contrived with dexterous carpentering and covered with black American leather, neatly finished off with brass-headed nails, and divisions put in to hold music books'.

It was while the sisters were doing this sorting out that Frances said 'Marie, it has come over me this morning that I shall send all my jewellery [except for a brooch or two for daily use...memorials of her dear parents] to the Church Missionary Society'. It was a practical outworking of her words, 'Take my silver and my gold, Not a mite would I withhold,' and her comment in doing it was, 'I had no idea I had such a jeweller's shop, nearly fifty articles are being packed off...I never packed a box with such pleasure'.

In the Appendix at the end of *Memorials of Frances Ridley Havergal*, a letter is included which Maria wrote after Frances' death to the Secretary of the Church Pastoral-Aid Society:

> Having read a statement about the failing funds of the C.P.A.S. Frances had expressed a desire to send a gift of £50, but when the claims of some other Societies were so urgently laid before her she gave to them instead. But the longing also to help the noble and half-paid workers in the Church vineyard still weighed on her..."How I wish I could send off a cheque at once! but fear I must wait a year." But as with other generous gifts, she waited not, but with much delight told me that she would give her much-valued piano, left to her by her beloved father...

A gift of £50 from the sale of the piano was later received by the Society, sent by her sister.

Following all this activity, Maria and Frances needed some quiet rest. When thinking of where to go they recalled the pleasant time they had spent in Wales near the Mumbles and decided to return there for the winter.

They enjoyed a stay with friends and came back to Pyrmont Villa, their parents' home in Leamington, to finish the task of clearing the home. On their last evening Frances sent for a number of her 'night-school boys' and gave them baskets of books and magazines, maps for their library, a magic lantern [19th century equivalent of a film projector or a power point presentation in the 21st century] and other articles which she thought would be useful to them. The boys never forgot the way she gathered them round her piano, sang with them 'Tell it Out' and gave some 'bright farewell words'.

– The Mumbles, Swansea –

As they needed to find a 'cosy nest' to retire to, Frances suggested to her sister that they should go to the Mumbles—it had obviously become a special place to her. So they went, asking for special guidance of 'the King' as to the locality, and the house they should choose. Maria relates:

> 'That will not do, 'tis too grand', said dear F.R.H. when shown a sea–side villa; 'I want a little nest, where you and I can be quiet and happy together'.
>
> Up the hill, past a lovely view of the fine ruins of Oystermouth Castle, a mile away from the Mumbles…there is a country lane called Caswell Bay Road, close to the village of Newton. A little way back from the road stands a small white house, with a pretty garden in front, filled with the bluest of forget–me–nots in summer.

We would hardly regard it as being 'small', but compared with many rectories and Victorian villas it was (See photograph 19)! Having settled that it would be 'just the thing!' they arranged to take their lodgings there for the winter.

For the next few months Frances spent time visiting friends and family and early in October joined Maria in their Welsh retreat. To a friend, Frances commented, 'I don't think I ever felt more thankful and glad for anything than on reaching this quiet little nest. God has so graciously and perfectly met our special need'.

Another thought she expressed was that if she could entirely 'tell it out' how good God was to her 'the ink would boil in my pen'.

In fact, Frances so delighted in their surroundings that she and Maria decided to stay on, little knowing that within eight months or so, as Maria later said, 'for her were opened the King's own palace gates, and she entered her heavenly home'.

Because their arrival at Caswell Bay was earlier than expected, the rooms were carpetless and everything unprepared. But F.R.H. rose to the occasion, as Maria tells us:

> Never grumbling, but brightly setting things in order, with little elegant contrivances making the most of what she had, her hands seemed a fairy wand in transforming bare rooms and walls. 'Give me American cloth, bright nails, and a hammer, and you will see, Marie!' So our rough packing boxes were made into music-stands and tidies. How I wish she could have been photographed as the merry carpenter, dovetailing and contriving!

- *Frances' Study* -

A description of her study presents her desk as having a most orderly arrangement of all her letters from editors, friends, the many requests she received, manuscripts etc. Even paper and string had their place and no litter was allowed. (Andrew Bonar was known to have said, 'Untidiness is unchristian'.) That must have been the only way she was able to cope with the multitude of different projects she was involved in. There seemed to have never been any lull in her life, as Frances once wrote:

> Rest! There is none for me apparently. Every post brings more letters from strangers alone...It is nine months since I have had a chance of doing a stroke of new work! But letters were a trouble to Nehemiah as well as to me (Neh. 6:4), and I must try to make it always work for my King.

Frances would work at her desk with little respite in order to keep abreast of all the letters etc. that kept flowing in. As Maria said to a friend after Frances had died, 'In heaven there is no post!'

The following list which came by one post will show what labour was required in dealing with them all:

> Request for contribution to Irish Church Advocate. Hymns for special New Year services wanted. To write cards suitable for mourners. For set of six more 'Marching Orders'. Request for poems to illustrate six pictures. For prayer, sympathy and counsel...Two sheets from a septuagenarian, requiring thought. Request to write a book suitable for Unitarians. Sundry inquiries and apologies from one who had been printing her verses with another's name. Request to reprint an article, with four explanatory enclosures. Also to revise a proof and add my opinion. To revise many sheets of musical manuscripts. Three requests to supply cards for bazaars. Advice wanted how to get articles inserted in magazines. To recommend pupils. To promote a new magazine. To give opinion on an oratorio. Some long poems in manuscript to revise and advise thereon. Besides packets of leaflets and cards wanted.

Is it any wonder that Frances' strength was tested to the limit and beyond!

A list of 'Work for 1879: If the Lord will' was found in her desk later and revealed how much work she had hoped to do through the year. Some was accomplished but much was left undone. One of the entries was 'Prepare "Kept" for the press', which she was able to do. This was a little book she wrote entitled *Kept for the Master's Use*. It was an expanded application of her 'Consecration Hymn', 'Take My Life.' She knew from the testimonies she had received that this hymn had been a blessing to many, and this book was written to encourage those who had given themselves and all that they had to the Saviour to go on to greater holiness.

When first published there was great demand for it, and it was to prove almost as popular as the hymn itself. Many thousands were printed and reprinted. Frances takes each couplet of the hymn and changes the one word *Take* to *Keep* and is fearless in her challenge to the reader, though always with a loving heart. Her comment in writing to a friend about it was:

> I have set really to work. I am re-writing part of the *Kept* papers: the first chapter is quite new; there was so much to say. It is a very serious thing to set about work which goes to tens of thousands. I felt I must set apart a day entirely for prayer, etc., which I did yesterday, instead of setting to work, and I do not think it was time lost.

In *Memorials* Maria quotes an extract from a letter of the Baroness Wrewsky, Golubowo, Russia, November 1879:

> I am just delighting in *Kept for the Master's Use*, and thank you so much for sending it. It is so full of earnest, realizing faith and love in Jesus, that it quite stirs one's heart to the very depth.

– A Visit to London –

Early in February 1879 Frances spent a fortnight in London. The main object of her visit was to see the publishers of her works, Mr. Watson and Mr. Robertson of Nisbet & Co., and Mr. Hutchings and Mr. Romer who were the publishers of her music. It was partly on the Rev. S. G. Prout's account that she went to see the latter two gentlemen, as she was hoping to negotiate the publication of his verses 'Loving all along'—written at the end of his book *Never Say Die* and set to her own music. To her delight they approved the suggestion, and also welcomed a number of her own hymns and tunes.

Nisbet was Frances' primary publisher: they published a great amount of her work, not only while she was alive but also after her death.

During this last visit to London she told her sister Maria that she had a very pressing offer of marriage, and that it was difficult to shake off the 'pure and holy love laid at her feet'. Maria recounts in her *Autobiography*:

> I may now say my sister bravely and unreservedly severed a correspondence and friendship which, though it scathed her heart, brought her into the fullest joy of being henceforth 'only for Jesus'. This bitter fruit yielded an afterwards of exceeding sweetness, and enabled her to counsel others who were tempted with the golden chain of matrimony under the delusion that they might win their beloved one to Christ. 'Only in the Lord' was my sister's safe rule and practice.

Frances herself confided to a friend:

> it is not...entirely feeling disappointed about ——, but more, I think, the sense of general heart-loneliness and need of a one and special love, ...and the belief that my life is to be a lonely one in that respect. ...I do so long for the love of Jesus to be poured in, as a real and satisfying compensation. ...I do so want Him to sanctify the whole thing, and give me spiritual blessing in and by it.

Her remaining time of total dedication and service to her Saviour proved how that desire was fulfilled in her life.

Does the following poem echo her thoughts at this time?

ENOUGH

I am so weak, dear Lord, I cannot stand
    One moment without Thee!
But oh! The tenderness of Thine enfolding,
And oh! The faithfulness of Thine upholding,
And oh! The strength of Thy right hand!
    That strength is enough for me!

I am so needy, Lord, and yet I know
    All fullness dwells in Thee;
And hour by hour that never-failing treasure
Supplies and fills, in overflowing measure,
My least, and greatest need, and so
    Thy grace is enough for me!

It is so sweet to trust Thy word alone:
I do not ask to see
The unveiling of Thy purpose, or the shining
Of future light on mysteries untwining:
Thy promise-roll is all my own –
Thy word is enough for me!

The human heart asks love, but now I know
That my heart hath from Thee
All real, and full, and marvellous affection,
So near, so human, yet divine perfection
Thrills gloriously the mighty glow!
Thy love is enough for me!

There were strange soul-depths, restless, vast, and broad,
Unfathomed as the sea;
An infinite craving for some infinite stilling,
But now Thy perfect love is perfect filling!
Lord Jesus Christ, my Lord, my God,
Thou, Thou art enough for me!

(Twenty-First Day of *Loyal Responses*)

On her return from this London visit, which was the last to her publishers, she threw herself into the various activities that she had become involved in since her arrival in Wales. These included ongoing work with the Bruey Branch of the Irish Society, some Bible lessons and hymn-singing in Newton school, as well as visiting the cottages in the area. Frances was, in fact, a frequent visitor to this Newton school, and to encourage the children to learn God's Word perfectly, offered a new Bible to every child who could repeat Isaiah 53. She was delighted with the perfect repetition by many of them.

Maria gave this account in her *Autobiography* of a day 'when we had taken donkeys to Bishoptown valley, and dismissed them at the school and church. In the churchyard a mother was crying while putting flowers on her daughter's grave. I do not know all that F. said to her, but she gently placed her hand on her shoulder with "Think of the meeting, not of the parting"'. Such was Frances' sympathetic and sensitive feelings for others.

It is interesting to note that Frances' presence is still remembered in the Newton area of Mumbles. In a report (which appeared in the Evangelical Times, June 2006) of the induction of a new minister into the Congregational Church in Mumbles, it was mentioned that F.R.H. had taught in the Sunday School and women's classes in the church there.

– *The Temperance Movement* –

Her sister Maria had seen the appalling results of drunkenness in Bewdley, in the parish of Worcester, when she was living there, and had been an active supporter of the Temperance Movement. But Frances had not been so easy to convince until 'conviction gradually dawned and deepened in my mind that I could not hold aloof from a movement on which God has set so very evident a seal of blessing'. On May 1, 1879 she wrote:

> I haven't taken up teetotal work, but teetotal work has taken up me! Morgan and Scott made me accept a big, handsome, pledge book in February, and somehow the thing has fairly caught fire here. One led to another, and yesterday boys were coming all day to sign! I had twenty-five recruits yesterday alone, and a whole squad more are coming this evening! And we are going in for getting EVERY boy in the whole village [Newton].

The boys, however, saw no reason for this sex discrimination, and with their protest: 'Please, miss, mayn't the girls sign?' Frances found herself then having to open a girls' branch as well. As the boys formed a most enthusiastic majority, Frances decided to give her band a martial title, 'The Newton Temperance Regiment'. Some seven years later, Maria was visiting in the district and came across the father of one of the lads who told her that even threats had failed to shake his son's loyalty: 'A man held brandy and water to him, and a knife, and said he would cut his throat if he didn't drink it, but Ben kept his pledge'. It would seem that at least some grew up to be men of sterling Christian character and useful in different spheres of life.

Also in May 1879 (just before her death) she wrote that 'All the rising generation have joined the pledge except about 12, and now the men want to speak to me...I have got 118 pledged, and each with a prayer over it and personal talk about better things'.

She had promised to meet some men and boys on the village bank later that month and, taking her Bible and Temperance book with her, went to keep her promise. It was wet and cold but she spoke to them all. On her way home from church the next day she was feeling very tired and was persuaded to have a donkey ride home. As she passed through the village quite a procession gathered round her, her regiment of boys eagerly listening. Her donkey boy, Fred, remembered that Miss Frances told him:

> I had better leave the devil's side and get on the safe side; that Jesus Christ's was the winning side; that He loved us and was calling us and wouldn't I choose Him for my Captain?

Arriving home, Frances ran in for her book and on the saddle Fred signed the pledge!

A young sailor was going to sea the next day and Frances went to his cottage to speak to him. He signed the book and listened to a message from her: his last letter from Brazil said that he had faithfully kept the pledge and remembered the words she had spoken to him.

To give some idea of the conditions prevailing in the Victorian era there is a story concerning a certain Frederick Charrington—the son of a partner in the brewery firm of Charrington and Head. A business career with a major fortune was his for the asking. In 1869, while in the south of France, he was thoroughly converted as he read the story of Nicodemus to please a friend. On his return to London, he began to visit a little mission hall each evening; the way led him past a beer shop called 'The Rising Sun'. One night as he passed by, he saw a poor woman with her children dragging at her skirts push open the door, and beg her husband 'for some money because the children were crying for bread'. That man's only reply was to knock her down and leave her in the gutter.

At that moment Charrington glanced up and saw his own name staring him in the face. 'Charrington, Head & Co's Entire' was written in large letters on the signboard. It flashed through his mind that this was one house out of thousands for which they were responsible. 'In knocking down his wife', he was to write, 'the man knocked me out of the liquor trade'. It was the great turning point in his life; it led him to renounce an income of £20,000 a year and a fortune of £250,000 in order to devote himself to work for Christ in the slums of London.

One can almost hear Frances saying, with her usual enthusiasm, 'Wonderful! Marvellous! Another victory for our King'!

Life in the Victorian era was very different from that of the 21st century. No National Health Service, no television or computers or iPods etc.! For many, just poverty, child slavery, or abuse of alcohol and short life expectancy. No wonder Frances' heart was stirred to do something, by God's grace, for the young people around her, to keep them from at least some of these evils.

RHYMED MOTTOES FOR THE MEMBERS OF THE OPEN-AIR MISSION

'Occupy till I return';
Let us, Lord, this lesson learn;
May our every moment be
Faithfully filled up for Thee.

'He that winneth souls is wise'
In the Master's gracious eyes;
Well may we contented be
To be counted fools for Thee.

So may we redeem the time,
That with every evening chime
Our rejoicing hearts may see
Blood–bought souls brought back to Thee.

(first, fourth, and fifth mottoes; *Life Echoes*)

– *Visits from Friends* –

Despite their busy life, the sisters were always pleased to welcome visitors. Among those who came was Elizabeth Clay who had been a very dear friend of Frances' ever since their school days. They had always kept in contact and Frances rejoiced that Elizabeth had been called to serve the Lord in India. So when she came home on furlough from the Punjab, it was natural that the two friends would want to meet and catch up on all the news.

A close friend of Maria and Frances was Baroness Helga von Cramm, whom they met on their visit to Switzerland in 1876. The Baroness was a gifted artist whose two specialities were Alpine scenery and the tiny Alpine flowers, and her drawings were used to illustrate some of Frances' works, including cards on which Frances had texts printed. She had joined them in early May 1879 and thought Frances was looking well when she left on the 24th of that month. None of them had any idea at that time that it would be the last meeting for Frances and the Baroness.

Mr. and Mrs. Ira D. Sankey also visited them. With their mutual interest in music, discussion of hymns was naturally a topic of conversation, though it was unfortunate that Frances was suffering from a cold and severe fever which left her almost voiceless and Sankey himself was on his way back to the States, unable to sing any more in England because of a severe throat infection.

On the day of their departure the Sankeys stopped at Newton school where they were met by a choir of children, led by Frances, singing 'Safe in the Arms of Jesus'. Mr Sankey got out of his carriage to thank them, and then Frances joined him and his wife in the carriage and drove with them a short way, leaving them at the bottom of the hill. His parting words to her, 'We'll meet again', received the response, 'Yes, if not here, in the bright city there!', and his last memory of her was the upward pointing finger and her waving handkerchief.

– Deepening Shadows –

Towards the end of May there was a return of the feverish attacks from which Frances had suffered previously, and the doctor diagnosed peritonitis. All remedies failed and when the doctor left he said goodbye; he did not anticipate that he would see her again. When she asked if he thought she was really going 'today', he said 'probably'. Her response was 'Splendid to be so near the gates of heaven'. She was heard repeatedly to say, 'Come, Lord Jesus, come and fetch me, Oh! run! run!'

We are given the details of her passing in *Memorials of Frances Ridley Havergal* by Maria:

> Towards one o'clock a.m. Whit–Tuesday, June 3rd, a change came… one of the sisters repeated, 'When thou passest through the waters, I will be with thee'. Frances immediately said, 'He must keep His word'. Another time, when she was in distressing pain, one of us began, 'Fear

thou not; for I am with thee' (Isaiah 41:10). But neither of us repeated it correctly—our darling, with her own accuracy, set us right.

Ellen repeated the words of one of her favourite hymns—'Jesus, I will trust Thee'—and clearly, though faintly, she sang the whole verse, to her own tune Hermas.

After another attack of sickness she said, 'There it is all over! Blessed rest!' And now she looked up steadfastly as if she saw the Lord...For ten minutes, we watched that almost visible meeting with her King, and her countenance was so glad, as if she were already talking to Him...as her brother commended her soul into her Redeemer's hand, she passed away.

Just three months previously she had given a friend the following lines, which seem to have anticipated her call to sudden glory:

PRECIOUS THINGS

Precious, precious to Jehovah is His children's holy sleep:
He is with them in the passing through the waters cold and deep;
Everlasting love enfolds them, softly, sweetly to His breast,
Everlasting love receives them to His glory and His rest.

(fifteenth stanza; *Under His Shadow*)

The text which had meant so much to her in life was to be her comfort in death—'The blood of Jesus Christ His Son cleanseth us from all sin'. Frances asked for this to be engraved on her gravestone. On Whit Monday, the day before she died, she whispered to a friend, 'There is no bottom to God's mercy and love! His promises are true, not one thing hath failed'.

And so on Tuesday, June 3rd, Frances was received up into glory.

On Monday, June 9, 1879 her mortal remains were laid to rest in the family vault in Astley churchyard: many relatives, friends and villagers assembled to give thanks for a life so full of blessing to very many and to rejoice in that sure and certain hope of her 'resurrection to eternal life'.

A marble tomb was later erected bearing the inscription:

FRANCES RIDLEY HAVERGAL
Youngest Daughter of the Rev. W.H. Havergal
and Jane his wife
Born at Astley Rectory, 14th December, 1836
Died at Caswell Bay, Swansea, 3rd June, 1879

Aged 42 years
By her writings in prose and verse, she, being
'dead, yet speaketh'.
'The blood of Jesus Christ His Son cleanseth
us from all sin'—1 John 1:7

*   *   *   *   *   *

In closing this story of one who was so devoted to her Saviour and King we quote from her grand 'Ascension Song', for which she wrote the tune 'Hermas':

ASCENSION SONG

Golden harps are sounding,
 Angel voices ring,
Pearly gates are opened –
 Opened for the King;
Christ, the King of glory,
 Jesus, King of love,
Is gone up in triumph
 To His throne above.
  All His work is ended,
   Joyfully we sing,
  Jesus hath ascended!
   Glory to our King!

He who came to save us,
 He who bled and died,
Now is crowned with glory
 At His Father's side.
Never more to suffer,
 Never more to die,
Jesus, King of glory,
 Is gone up on high.
  All His work is ended,
   Joyfully we sing,
  Jesus hath ascended!
   Glory to our King!

Praying for His children,
 In that blessed place,
Calling them to glory,

Sending them His grace;
His bright home preparing,
Faithful ones, for you;
Jesus ever liveth,
Ever loveth too.
All His work is ended,
Joyfully we sing,
Jesus hath ascended!
Glory to our King!

(*Under the Surface*)

Chapter Fourteen

Frances Ridley Havergal's Legacy

What is the legacy that Frances has left us? She was, above all, a woman of true spirituality and the love of Jesus was the guiding principle throughout her life. Her constant and deep study of the Scriptures, together with her memorization of them, gave Frances a breadth of knowledge which she was able to bring to all her writings, as well as use in her personal contacts and conversations. Linked with her love of the Bible, there was also a deep inner life of prayer and dependence on Jesus Christ for guidance in all things. Thus she has left us an example to spur us on to seek a deeper knowledge of God's Word, a greater devotion in prayer, and a desire to tell others the good news of the gospel.

Frances has also left us her hymns which have been a blessing to the Church to this day. A selection has been given in chapter eight, but there are many more which could have been included. 'Time would fail me to tell' of them all.

Her concern for the well–being, both materially and spiritually, of the poor she visited in the Almshouses and cottages in her father's parishes, as well as her determination to sing only for Jesus in the 'tea-meetings' held among the society of her day, emphasised her practical outlook and her dedication to her Master.

The overall impression gained through reading almost all her works that were made available to me (nearly five thousand pages), was that Frances was a bright yet humble Christian, spreading joy and love wherever she went, commending her Saviour and proving by her life and death the reality of her experience of a consecrated life.

A WORKER'S PRAYER

'None of us liveth unto himself'
(Romans 14:7)

Lord, speak to me, that I may speak
   In living echoes of Thy tone;
As Thou hast sought, so let me seek
   Thy erring children, lost and lone.

O lead me, Lord, that I may lead
   The wandering and the wavering feet;
O feed me, Lord, that I may feed
   Thy hungering ones with manna sweet.

O strengthen me, that while I stand
   Firm on the Rock and strong in Thee,
I may stretch out a loving hand
   To wrestlers with the troubled sea.

O teach me, Lord, that I may teach
   The precious things Thou dost impart;
And wing my words, that they may reach
   The hidden depths of many a heart.

O give Thine own sweet rest to me,
   That I may speak with soothing power
A word in season, as from Thee,
   To weary ones in needful hour.

O fill me with Thy fulness, Lord,
   Until my very heart o'erflow
In kindling thought and glowing word,
   Thy love to tell, Thy praise to show.

O use me, Lord, use even me,
   Just as Thou wilt, and when, and where;
Until Thy blessed Face I see,
   Thy rest, Thy joy, Thy glory share.

(Under the Surface)

When she sang on her deathbed, 'Thou hast died for sinners, Therefore, Lord for me', she was voicing the truth of her conviction and her response to the Saviour's love.

As in life, so in death: may we seek to follow her example, 'Looking unto Jesus, the author and finisher of our faith' (Heb. 12:2).

GRANTED
MINISTRIES
— PRESS —

WHAT YOU CAN AFFORD POLICY

As with all of the resources that we make available, this book is offered to any who believe they can benefit from it, whether they can pay for it or not. There is a cost for the book, but we do not want this to be an obstacle to anyone. If you cannot afford to purchase a copy, or if you can only afford a portion of the price, we ask that you write and give us the opportunity to serve God by providing for His people. Our only stipulation is that you not request the book unless you are certain to read it within six months. We do not want to generously enlarge your library, but to generously enlarge your spiritual condition.

−**C.T.** *October, 2009*

GRANTED MINISTRIES PRESS
P.O. Box 1348
Hannibal, MO 63401-1348
www.grantedministries.org

Other Titles Available from Granted Ministries Press

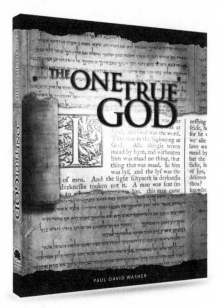

The One True God by Paul D. Washer
Hardcover: 7.4" x 9.5"
Page Count: 192
ISBN: 9780981732107

A unique kind of workbook, *The One True God* intends not just to teach truth but to lead to an encounter with the living God. Beneath that goal the book aims to ground believers in orthodox Christian theology and the actual contents of the Bible. Students are encouraged to thoughtfully draw conclusions from the *Scriptures* rather than to merely absorb the principles, inferences, and illustrations set before them by the *author*. For this reason the book does not include such material and instead focuses on digesting the Scriptures directly. This workbook is the finest resource for new converts of which we are aware.

This book is essentially bound as a Wire-O bound journal, with a hardback cover wrapping around the entire book, even the spine. This keeps the book in good shape for a long time, and also provides for optimum usability.

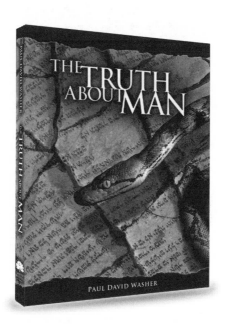

The Truth About Man by Paul D. Washer
Hardcover: 7.4" x 9.5"
Page Count: 176
ISBN: 9780981732114

This workbook is set up just like *The One True God*, focusing on digesting the Scriptures directly. Readers will find the book invaluable. While of extreme importance to the believer, the biblical witness concerning the condition of man is often misunderstood or ignored. This workbook is a wonderful help in seeking a remedy.

This book is essentially bound as a Wire-O bound journal, with a hardback cover wrapping around the entire book, even the spine. This keeps the book in good shape or a long time, and provides for optimum usability.

Valuable Selections from the Writings of George Müller
Paperback: 5.5" x 8.5"
Page Count: 64
ISBN: 9780981732138

Valuable Selections from the Writings of George Müller is a collection of writings compiled by Paul Washer for the impact they have had upon himself, and the direction of HeartCry Missionary Society, which he directs. These writings have been especially helpful to countless believers. This booklet includes Müller's testimony, his teachings on subjects such as faith, the kingdom and its treasures, stewardship, partnership with God, the study of Scripture, and discerning the will of God. Also read Müller's encouragement to those with unconverted family members; an address once given to young converts regarding the importance of the Word of God; and several excerpts from his journal of God's abundant provision in the midst of, and out of, various trials. After a few pages explaining why Müller desired to begin the orphan houses, the book concludes with a final exhortation to prayer.

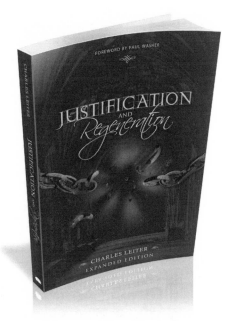

Justification and Regeneration by Charles Leiter

English Edition:
Paperback: 5.5" x 8.5"
Page Count: 192
ISBN: 9780981732152

Spanish Edition:
Paperback: 5.5" x 8.5"
Page Count: 176
ISBN: 9780981732121

What does the Bible mean when it says that Christians have "died to sin"? How is it possible for a just God to "justify the ungodly" without becoming "unjust" Himself? What is regeneration? What is justification? Why do all men desperately need to be justified? If I have died to sin, why am I still affected by it? As a Christian, am I the "new man" or the "old man"—or both? What does the Bible mean when it says that Christians have "died to the law"? Are Christians still slaves to sin?

The answers to these and many other questions become clear once we gain a biblical understanding of justification and regeneration. These two great miracles lie at the very heart of the gospel, yet even among genuine Christians they are surrounded by confusion and ignorance. This book attempts to set forth in clear biblical light the nature and characteristics of justification and regeneration that God may be glorified and His children brought to know more fully the liberty that is theirs in Christ.

VALUABLE SELECTIONS FROM THE WRITINGS OF
FRANCES RIDLEY HAVERGAL

Valuable Selections from the Writings of Frances Ridley Havergal
Paperback: 5.5" x 8.5"
Page Count: 96
ISBN: 9780981732183

Frances Ridley Havergal (1836-1879) was born a pastor's daughter. Her father sacrificed in order to provide a fine education for his children. Frances' formal education ended at 17, with one term at a young woman's school in Germany, where, for the first time in its history, the school awarded a student first prize, Frances being the recipient of that award. Having surrendered her heart to the Lord at 14, she viewed her knowledge as a means to know Christ more, and to make Him more known.

This selection of her work is reflective of the quality of virtually all her writing. The first half of the book is a collection of sixty very fine poems, diligently arranged to dove-tail from one poem and topic to the next. This is followed by several excerpts from her letters, and ten challenging and helpful prose pieces. The booklet then concludes with six of her music scores. It is our hope that this booklet will be of service to our King—both in the growth of His bride and the expanse of His kingdom.